MADE E

# 101 INTERESTING STORIES

## about *EVERYTHING*

**Incredibly Cool Stories About History, Discoveries, Wars, Sports, Nature, People, and More for Curious Minds**

Producer & International Distributor
eBookPro Publishing
www.ebook-pro.com

**101 Interesting Stories About Everything:** Incredibly Cool Stories About History, Discoveries, Wars, Sports, Nature, People, and More for Curious Minds

Made Easy Press

Contact: agency@ebook-pro.com
ISBN 9798866037797

# CONTENTS

#  INTRODUCTION

Hello there, and welcome to a magical, fascinating world of true stories that will amaze you!

Dive into the world of scientific discoveries to find out how the Post-It, microwave oven, and popsicles were invented.

Explore unexplained mysteries like the lost colony of Roanoke, The Wow! Signal from space, and the vanishing village of Angikuni.

Meet incredible animal friends who survived disasters, revolutionized science, and saved lives.

Get to know inspiring people with truly unbelievable life stories, from unbeatable athletes and medical marvels to human lightning rods and kids who grew up with wolves.

Discover compelling natural phenomena such as pink watermelon snow, beautiful fire rainbows, and captivating bubbles trapped under ice.

Immerse yourself in creepy crimes that will leave you with goosebumps.

And go back in time to learn about the hilarious, miraculous, and monumental moments that changed the course of history.

*101 Interesting Stories About Everything* makes learning new things a fun, exciting, and educational experience. So kick back, sit down, and prepare to amaze your friends and family with all the fascinating things you will learn!

## THE DISCOVERY OF PENICILLIN

In the annals of medical history, a pivotal moment changed the trajectory of modern medicine. Alexander Fleming, a brilliant scientist, inadvertently unearthed a groundbreaking discovery that would eventually shape the course of medical treatment worldwide – the antibiotic known as penicillin.

In an era when laboratories were abuzz with scientific inquiry, Fleming worked diligently in his laboratory, studying bacteria and conducting experiments. One fateful day, he accidentally left a petri dish containing a colony of bacteria exposed on his workbench. A gust of wind carried a minuscule mold spore into his lab through an open window, and fate intervened.

In the days that followed, Fleming observed a curious phenomenon around the mold-infested area of the petri dish. It was as if the bacteria surrounding the mold were retreating. Upon closer examination, Fleming realized that the mold secreted a substance with the remarkable ability to counteract the bacteria.

This discovery set the wheels of scientific inquiry in motion. Fleming named the newfound substance "penicillin," and his passion for understanding its potential drove him to unravel its therapeutic properties. Collaborating with fellow researchers, he tirelessly explored methods to harness penicillin's capabilities to combat infections.

Imagine an army of microscopic warriors primed to engage in battle against microscopic adversaries – an analogy that perfectly captures penicillin's role in fighting pathogenic organisms responsible for causing illnesses. This revolutionary antibiotic attacked harmful bacteria, saving countless lives in the process.

The ripple effect of this discovery reverberated globally. The collective efforts of scientists transcended borders, culminating in the production of penicillin on a grand scale. As its application expanded, penicillin's impact on medical treatment became increasingly evident. It offered a lifeline to patients battling infections that once posed grave threats to their well-being.

Alexander Fleming's inquisitive mind unlocked the potential of a tiny mold spore, leading to an innovation that revolutionized the field of medicine. The story of penicillin underscores the importance of meticulous research, collaboration, and the relentless pursuit of knowledge.

## BABY WOOLLY MAMMOTH

Deep within the frozen lands of Canada, a group of gold miners stumbled upon a treasure that transported them back in time. These miners, with their picks and shovels, were on a mission to find precious gold, hidden beneath the icy frost. Little did they know, their digging would uncover something much more incredible than gold.

As they chipped away at a wall of frozen earth, a surprising sight caught their eyes. A bundle of ancient fur and skin emerged from the ground, revealing the remains of a real-life baby mammoth, frozen in time for thousands of years.

As the miners realized the significance of their discovery, they stopped their work immediately, understanding that this was a once-in-a-lifetime find.

Scientists and researchers carefully studied the baby mammoth, eager to learn about her life from so long ago. They believed she was just a month old when she met her fate.

What's truly mind-blowing is that this little mammoth still had her skin, fur, and even her toenails preserved. It's as if the icy permafrost wrapped her up in a frozen hug, protecting her for all these years.

But the story doesn't end there. The baby mammoth was about to receive a special gift from the present day. The Tr'ondëk Hwëch'in elders, wise members of the Yukon First Nation, decided to bless her with a name. They called her "Nun cho ga," which means "big baby animal." They honored her presence and connected her to the land they call home.

An unsuspecting group of gold miners, seeking treasures from the Earth, unearthed a treasure of history itself—a baby woolly mammoth named Nun Cho ga. She takes us back in time to a world long ago, where these magnificent creatures roamed the Earth alongside ancient humans. Thanks to the frozen permafrost, we can catch a glimpse of the past and marvel at the wonders of our planet

## THE HISTORY OF POST-ITS

In 1980, an inventive mind named Spencer Silver was hard at work, trying to create a super-strong glue. However, his concoction had a whimsical twist – it turned out to be not-so-sticky! But in the world of creativity, mistakes often unveil hidden treasures.

One day, another bright mind named Art Fry was grappling with a frustration that many students and office workers know well: his bookmarks kept falling out of his choir hymnal. Little did he know that the solution to his dilemma was brewing just a few desks away.

Enter Spencer Silver's "not-so-sticky" adhesive. Fry quickly realized that this peculiar adhesive had a unique charm – it stuck lightly, allowing for easy removal without leaving a gooey trace. He saw a way to solve his bookmark problem while creating something entirely new.

Fry started using bits of paper treated with Silver's adhesive to mark pages in his hymnal. The pieces held in place without damaging the pages, making them ideal bookmarks. He shared his discovery with his colleagues, and soon, everyone in the office was using these little paper marvels to jot down reminders and leave notes for one another.

Their accidental invention caught the attention of their employer, 3M, a company known for innovation. Recognizing the potential of this simple yet ingenious creation, they refined the design, adding bright colors and a catchy name: "Post-it Notes."

## WHERE DID CHEWING GUM COME FROM?

Long ago, when ancient civilizations roamed the earth, there was a group of people known as the Maya, who lived in what is now Mexico and Central America. These resourceful folks were ahead of their time when it came to crafting everyday wonders.

In the midst of their bustling lives, the Maya discovered something curious: a gum-like substance oozing from sapodilla trees. Instead of discarding it, they decided to investigate. They realized that when they chewed this sticky treasure, it transformed into something quite enjoyable. Little did they know that their playful experimentation would become the foundation for a worldwide phenomenon.

Fast-forward to the 19th century, when a young inventor named Thomas Adams was on a quest to find an alternative use for a certain kind of rubber – a type that was neither bouncy nor stretchy enough for tires. Adams had heard about the Mayans' gum-chewing exploits and thought, why not give it a shot?

He began mixing the rubber with flavorings, creating small chunks of what he called "chewing gum." Unfortunately, his rubbery concoction didn't become the next big thing in the tire industry, but it did pave the way for something far more delightful.

One day, Adams's gum found itself in the hands of a photographer named John Curtis. Curtis had the brilliant idea to sell Adams's gum in vending machines on train platforms. People could purchase this chewy treat and enjoy it during their travels. It was an instant hit!

People loved the chewy texture, and chewing gum quickly became a sensation. Gum manufacturers began experimenting with flavors and packaging, turning chewing gum into the colorful treat we know today.

The story of chewing gum is a testament to the power of curiosity, experimentation, and a dash of good luck. From the ancient Maya's exploration of tree sap to Thomas Adams's rubbery creations, and finally, to John Curtis's accidental revelation – each chapter contributed to the sweet story of chewing gum's journey from nature to delighting taste buds around the world.

## ARCHIMEDES AND EUREKA!

In the ancient city of Syracuse lived a brilliant mind named Archimedes. A man of both thought and action, he was a renowned scientist and mathematician whose insights still influence our world today. Among his many achievements, one discovery stands out – the principle of buoyancy.

Archimedes was tasked with distinguishing whether a gold crown was truly composed of pure gold or if cunning individuals had attempted to deceive by using an inferior metal.

Amid his quest for solutions, Archimedes took solace in his bathtub, a place where he often found respite from the demands of his work. That fateful day, as he immersed himself in the water, a peculiar phenomenon caught his attention. He observed that the water level in the tub rose as he entered it. This seemingly mundane observation set the wheels of his intellect into motion.

Archimedes recognized the significance of this incident, prompting him to explore the underlying principles at play. With meticulous consideration, he realized that his body's entry into the water displaced a volume of water equal to his own mass. This understanding led him to the groundbreaking insight that an object submerged in a fluid experiences an upward force known as buoyancy. The more the object displaces the fluid, the greater the buoyant force it encounters.

Enthralled by his revelation, Archimedes leaped from his bathtub, exclaiming the word "Eureka!" which in Greek means "I have found it!" His excitement was not merely for himself, but for the scientific community and the world at large. His discovery, while rooted in the simple act of immersion, held profound implications for understanding the behaviors of objects in fluids.

The story of Archimedes and his discovery of buoyancy serves as a reminder that groundbreaking insights often arise from unexpected places and circumstances. Archimedes's ability to perceive the profound within the ordinary underscores the importance of observation, analysis, and a tenacious pursuit of understanding.

## MARIE CURIE AND RADIOACTIVITY

In the early 20th century, as the world teemed with scientific exploration, a Polish scientist named Marie Curie embarked on a quest that would illuminate the depths of the atomic realm. She was captivated by the mysterious phenomenon of radioactivity – the emission of rays from certain elements that could penetrate matter. Curie sought to unveil the enigma of these rays and their implications for the scientific community.

Amid the quiet corridors of her laboratory, Curie delved into her research with a determination that would ultimately change the course of modern science. She meticulously investigated various materials, particularly the element uranium, known for its unique properties. Through countless experiments, Curie discovered that uranium emitted rays spontaneously, without any external stimulation.

As she explored further, she uncovered a profound revelation: not only did uranium emit rays, but so did another element – thorium. This unexpected discovery challenged every existing notion about the stability of matter. Curie's findings led her to coin the term "radioactivity" to describe this astonishing property possessed by select elements.

In her pursuit of knowledge, Curie did not shy away from the hazardous nature of her investigations. She recognized that the rays emitted by radioactive materials could be perilous to human health, but she persevered in the face of challenges. Her relentless dedication led her to devise groundbreaking techniques for isolating radioactive elements, paving the way for their further study and application.

Although she later tragically died due to extensive exposure to radioactive substances, Marie Curie cemented her legacy in science and her discoveries have contributed to medical treatments, diagnostics, and energy production. Marie Curie was even awarded two Nobel Prizes for her work – one in physics and one in chemistry, making her the only woman to have won the prestigious prize in two different fields.

## A VERY UNIQUE COLOR

In mid-1800s London, a chemist named William Henry Perkin was immersed in his laboratory. At age 18, Perkin was on a mission to synthesize quinine, a remedy for malaria derived from the bark of cinchona trees. In a twist of fate, one of Perkin's experiments working with coal tar yielded an unexpected outcome – a vibrant purple solution.

The captivating color that emerged from Perkin's experiments was unlike any he had encountered before – a delicate and rich shade that resembled the petals of a flower.

Perkin recognized the commercial potential of his newfound color. He swiftly realized that this beautiful shade could be utilized as a textile dye, adding a new dimension to the realm of fashion and design. The color quickly caught the attention of designers and artists, igniting a trend that would come to define an era.

The name "mauve" was bestowed upon this mesmerizing pale blue-purple hue, a term derived from the French word "malva," meaning mallow flower. Its popularity spread like wildfire, transforming dresses, accessories, and interiors with its unique charm.

The ripple effect of Perkin's discovery extended beyond the fashion industry. Mauve served as a catalyst for further research into synthetic dyes, propelling the field of chemistry forward and revolutionizing the way colors were produced and perceived. This transformation laid the foundation for the modern world of color that we know today.

## THE X-RAY MISTAKE

Way back in the late 19th century, a physicist named Wilhelm Conrad Roentgen was navigating the frontiers of electricity and radiation. In his laboratory, he was experimenting with cathode rays, a type of invisible energy produced in a vacuum tube. Little did he know that his experiments would lead him to the discovery of something extraordinary.

One fateful day, as Roentgen observed the curious glow emitted by a cathode ray tube, he noticed a piece of paper coated with a fluorescent material that was lying nearby. The fluorescent material began to shimmer, even though it was not in direct contact with the tube. Intrigued, Roentgen was determined to uncover the source of this peculiar phenomenon.

As he continued his experiments, Roentgen realized that the fluorescent glow was not being caused by the cathode rays themselves, but by some other form of energy they were emitting. He labeled this mysterious energy "X-rays," a placeholder for the unknown.

Roentgen delved into further investigations, uncovering the astonishing ability of X-rays to penetrate substances that were opaque to ordinary light. The potential applications of this discovery became evident — it was as if a new form of vision had been bestowed upon humanity. Roentgen soon recognized that X-rays could be used to visualize the internal structures of objects, including, groundbreakingly, the human body.

In a historic moment that marked the convergence of science and medicine, Roentgen aimed his X-ray machine at his own hand and took an X-ray image. What appeared before his eyes was a detailed view of the bones within his hand — a feat that had never been achieved before. This moment paved the way for the field of medical radiography, forever altering the landscape of healthcare.

The revolutionary impact of Roentgen's discovery extended far beyond medicine. X-rays would later be applied in diverse fields, from materials testing to security screening. This newfound capability to peer into the hidden layers of reality marked a paradigm shift in human perception and revolutionized the way we diagnose and treat medical conditions.

# THE INVENTION
# OF THE MICROWAVE OVEN

In the mid-20th century, a scientist named Percy Spencer was fervently investigating the properties of magnetrons — devices used in radar systems during World War II. Spencer was working at the Raytheon Corporation, a company at the forefront of electronic innovation.

One day, as Spencer tinkered with a magnetron, he encountered an unexpected phenomenon. He had placed a chocolate bar in his pocket, which began unexpectedly to melt due to the heat generated by the magnetron. Intrigued by this peculiar occurrence, Spencer turned his inquisitive mind toward further experimentation.

With curiosity as his guide, Spencer conducted a series of experiments involving various food items. Placing an egg near the magnetron, he was astonished when it exploded, coating the entire lab in a mess of scrambled eggs.

Spencer realized that the magnetron emitted electromagnetic waves, which could penetrate and heat food items from the inside out. This insight marked the birth of the microwave oven – a device that harnessed the power of electromagnetic radiation for culinary applications.

Spencer refined the concept and developed the first microwave oven prototype. The revolutionary appliance was not only faster in terms of cooking time but was also far more convenient and efficient than the traditional oven.

Suddenly, people had the means to prepare and enjoy meals in a matter of minutes, a significant departure from the hours previously spent in kitchen labor.

The microwave oven found its place in households, workplaces, and even space exploration. Its applications ranged from reheating leftovers to the rapid preparation of frozen dinners. The appliance's success reaffirmed the power of accidental discoveries and the intersection of scientific inquiry with everyday life.

## THE VERY FIRST POPSICLE

One evening in 1905, an eleven-year-old boy named Frank Epperson was enjoying a glass of flavored soda water powder mixed with water. But before he could finish his drink, Frank got distracted and left his glass, with the stirring stick still inside, on his porch.

As fate would have it, an unexpectedly chilly night descended upon Frank's neighborhood, causing the mixture to freeze around the stirring stick. The young boy was astonished the next morning to find that the contents of his glass had transformed into a refreshing, frozen confection. He eagerly pulled the stick from the glass and took a lick, savoring the taste of a brand-new sensation.

Inspired by his discovery, Frank began sharing his newfound treat with friends and family. He called it the "Epsicle" — a combination of his own last name and the word "icicle." The sweet creation quickly gained popularity among those who tasted it, and it wasn't long before the name was simplified to the now-familiar "popsicle."

Frank's icy invention remained a cherished family treat for years. It wasn't until decades later, when he was an adult, that he realized the full potential of his accidental creation. In 1923, Frank patented the popsicle, kickstarting their commercial production. His journey from his family's porch to the world of business marked the transformation of a simple delight into a cultural phenomenon.

The popsicle's vibrant colors, array of flavors, and portability captured the imagination of young and old alike. From backyard barbecues to sunny picnics, it has become a symbol of carefree enjoyment and summertime pleasures.

## HOW A COW BECAME A VACCINE

The story of the first vaccine begins with a man named Edward Jenner, an English physician living in the late 18th century. During this time, smallpox was a severe and highly contagious disease that caused suffering and death across the globe.

Jenner noticed an interesting phenomenon: milkmaids who had contracted a mild illness called cowpox seemed to be immune to smallpox. Intrigued by this observation, Jenner conducted an experiment that would change the course of medical history.

In 1796, Jenner collected pus from a cowpox sore on a milkmaid and then used it to infect an 8-year-old boy named James. After a few days, James developed a mild case of cowpox but soon recovered.

Then, Jenner exposed James to smallpox, expecting the boy to fall seriously ill, as most children would. However, to Jenner's amazement, James did not develop smallpox; he was completely protected. This experiment provided the first evidence that cowpox could prevent smallpox.

Edward Jenner coined the term "vaccine" from the Latin word "vacca," which means "cow," to describe his revolutionary method. He called the substance created from cowpox the "vaccine virus."

The success of Jenner's smallpox vaccine paved the way for the development of vaccines against numerous other diseases, saving countless lives, preventing suffering, and revolutionizing medicine forever.

## HARDCORE HISTORY

### THE MOLASSES DISASTER

In January 1919, a large tank filled with over 2 million gallons of molasses stood in the North End neighborhood of Boston. Molasses, a thick and sticky syrup, was used to make rum and other products. On a fateful day, the tank suddenly burst open, releasing a massive wave of molasses traveling at speeds of up to 35 miles per hour right into the city center.

The molasses wave, estimated to be around 25 feet tall, surged through the streets, demolishing buildings, uprooting trees, and even knocking a train off its tracks. The force of the flood was so powerful that it swept people and animals off their feet and trapped them in a gooey mess.

The disaster was both shocking and tragic. Twenty-one people lost their lives, and many more were injured. Rescue efforts were made difficult by the sticky conditions. It took days for the city to clean up the aftermath, with firefighters and workers eventually using salt water to break down the molasses and wash it away.

The cause of the molasses tank's failure was attributed to a combination of factors, including temperature changes that may have caused the molasses to expand and contract, putting pressure on the tank's walls. The tank was also not properly constructed, with weak spots that contributed to the catastrophe.

The Great Molasses Flood led to stricter regulations for industrial facilities and a greater emphasis on safety standards. It also sparked a series of lawsuits and investigations to determine who was responsible for the tragedy.

# CHERNOBYL GHOST TOWN

On April 26, 1986, reactor number 4 at the Chernobyl Nuclear Power Plant in Ukraine exploded, releasing a massive cloud of radioactive particles into the atmosphere. The immediate impact was catastrophic – leading to the deaths of plant workers and emergency responders due to acute radiation exposure.

The disaster forced the evacuation of nearby towns and cities, displacing thousands of people. The radioactive cloud spread far beyond Ukraine, affecting neighboring countries and even reaching parts of Europe. The Chernobyl disaster is considered the worst nuclear accident in history.

In the aftermath, courageous firefighters and workers, known as "liquidators," risked their lives to contain the radiation and prevent further damage. They built a massive concrete sarcophagus, known as the "Chernobyl Shelter," to encase the damaged reactor and prevent the spread of more radioactive materials.

Today, the Chernobyl Exclusion Zone, a 1,000-square-mile area around the plant, remains off-limits to most humans due to high radiation levels. However, nature has started to reclaim the land. The absence of human activity has created a unique ecosystem, with plants and animals flourishing in the absence of human intervention. Wolves, deer, and even a small population of horses have made the zone their home.

Efforts to manage and mitigate the effects of the disaster continue. The New Safe Confinement, a massive steel structure, was constructed to cover the damaged reactor and contain any remaining radiation. The area around Chernobyl is now monitored to ensure the safety of both the environment and the people who work there.

# THE FIRST TIME CAPSULE

You've probably heard of the concept of a time capsule – you put some meaningful items into a cache and then store it away to be opened at a future date. It's a way for us to deliberately communicate with people in the future, and to leave behind some information about our period of history. But have you heard about the first modern time capsule?

In 1936, at Oglethorpe University in Atlanta, Georgia, a remarkable project was initiated. It was the brainchild of Dr. Thornwell Jacobs, the university's president, who had a vision to preserve a snapshot of civilization for generations way in the future to discover. This ambitious endeavor aimed to encapsulate the essence of human history and culture within a sealed chamber, which Jacobs named "The Crypt of Civilization."

The crypt, a 20 by 10 by 10-foot underground room, was constructed to withstand the test of time. It was filled with a huge array of items representing various aspects of human existence. From books and musical recordings to everyday household items, the crypt was a treasure trove of artifacts, designed to provide future generations with a realistic window into the past.

The crypt has never been opened since and very clear instructions state that it should only be opened 6,000 years from the day it was sealed. Just think how different the world will be in year 8,000 – and how fascinating future generations of humans will find our own mundane lives.

## NEW YORK'S SECRET SUBWAY

In the bustling streets of New York City in the 1870s, a secret project was about to reshape the city's transportation landscape forever. While the iconic modern subway system that we know today wasn't the first, its origins are intertwined with a tale of innovation, secrecy, and determination.

In the mid-19th century, the streets of New York were plagued by traffic congestion, particularly along the busy thoroughfare of Broadway. It was against this backdrop that Alfred Ely Beach, a young entrepreneur who owned the magazine Scientific American, conceived an audacious idea—an underground railway to alleviate the congestion.

Beach's concept was bold and unconventional. He envisioned a railcar that would be propelled by a massive fan, gliding through an underground tunnel. The innovation lay in the unique method of propulsion, very different from traditional steam-powered trains. But the path to turning this vision into reality was far from straightforward.

One major hurdle was the city's Commissioner of Public Works, William Tweed, whose influence and income were tied to existing transportation systems. To bypass Tweed's opposition, Beach hatched a clever strategy. He obtained permission to build the underground tunnel by disguising it as a mail delivery system. Then, Beach and a small team embarked on a clandestine project of digging an underground tunnel beneath Broadway, all under the cover of darkness.

Their work progressed diligently until word leaked to the press, making the underground endeavor public knowledge. With the project now out in the open, Beach and his team ramped up their efforts to complete the subway.

Finally, on March 1, 1870, Beach's underground rail made its grand debut. The line carried passengers from Warren Street to Murray Street, covering a short but significant stretch. The new mode of transportation was a hit, attracting over 400,000 passengers in its first year of operation.

However, Beach's success was met with resistance. William Tweed, outraged by the audacity of the underground rail, vetoed any extensions to the system. Tweed's reign of power eventually came to an end as he was imprisoned for corruption, paving the way for Beach to resume his work. Yet, as the economy began to falter, Beach faced dwindling investor support.

Tragically, Beach's ambitious plans were left unfinished, and the hidden subway remained sealed beneath the city's streets. The subway, complete with a luxury railcar and machinery, became a hidden piece of history. Today, it lies entwined with the present-day City Hall Station, a testament to Alfred Ely Beach's remarkable vision and the obstacles he faced.

So, the next time you descend into the depths of New York's bustling subway system, remember the hidden tale of Alfred Ely Beach and his underground rail. It's a story of innovation born from necessity, of determination that overcame secrecy, and of a glimpse into a past where transportation boundaries were pushed to unveil a new era of travel.

## TERRIFYING CIRCUS LION ATTACK

There was a time when circuses were a spectacle of wonder and danger lurked behind even the most innocent of acts. In the midst of grand parades and thrilling performances, a gruesome event unfolded that would forever change the way people looked at the circus band.

In the 19th century, the James Robinson Circus was a bustling circus procession making its way through the streets of towns, captivating audiences with the promise of awe-inspiring performances. Its manager had a daring idea to captivate the public's attention even before the main show began. The circus band would perform on a stage mounted atop the den of majestic Barbary lions, a sight that would surely leave the crowd in awe.

Despite repeated warnings about the precariousness of this setup, the idea was embraced. The promise of a thrilling spectacle drove the decision forward. As the circus rolled into towns, the band would serenade the audience from their perch atop the lions' den. The daring act proved successful, drawing intrigued crowds and sparking curiosity.

The fateful morning of the incident arrived in 1870, when the circus made its way to Middletown, Kansas. The parade through the streets began, and the band took their place on the stage above the cage that housed the Barbary lions. But as fate would have it, a mishap occurred. The leading carriages became entangled, creating chaos and panic in the procession. Amidst the turmoil, disaster struck – the driver of the lion cage lost control, colliding with a rock. The impact was so forceful that it caused the braces supporting the stage to collapse, sending the entire band plummeting straight into the lions' den.

The lions, startled and agitated, attacked the fallen band members in front of a shocked audience. The once-tame act turned into a nightmare as the musicians faced the fury of the fierce predators.

The outcome was nothing short of tragic. Out of the ten musicians, three lost their lives on the spot. Four others, despite being taken to safety, succumbed to their injuries later.

Adding to the tragedy, even the alpha lion known as Old Nero was not spared from the chaos. In the midst of the rescue mission, he attacked his keeper, prompting the sad decision to put down the once-majestic creature.

So, the next time you hear the joyful notes of a circus tune, remember the brave musicians who took an unexpected step into the lions' den.

## THE ROCKETGRAM

Picture yourself in the 1930s, a time when people were captivated by the possibilities of flight and space exploration. Enter Friedrich Schmiedl, an Austrian engineer who dreamt of revolutionizing mail delivery. Schmiedl's vision? To launch mail into the air using rockets and have it descend safely back to Earth, all while delighting recipients with the novelty of a "rocketgram."

Schmiedl's dream was put into action in 1931, when he designed a rocket capable of carrying mail. The rocket was equipped with a compartment to hold letters and postcards, and it was fitted with fins for stability during flight. Excitement buzzed through the air as the world waited to witness the first rocket-powered mail delivery.

The historic moment arrived on February 23, 1931, in the Austrian town of St. Georgen am Steinfeld. A crowd gathered to witness Schmiedl's experiment as the rocket was ignited, propelling the mail into the sky with a burst of fiery energy. As the rocket soared upward, cheers erupted from the onlookers.

The rocket successfully reached an altitude of around 90 meters before its engine cut out. The mail compartment detached from the rocket and floated gently back to the ground using a parachute. The crowd watched in awe as the mail gracefully descended, a triumph of engineering and imagination.

Schmiedl's experiment captured the imagination of the world, and rocket mail gained popularity as a novel way to send messages. However, the practicality of rocket mail faced challenges. Rockets were often unpredictable and posed safety risks, and weather conditions could impact their trajectory. As a result, rocket mail remained a daring yet unreliable method of mail delivery.

Even so, various countries, including Germany and the United States, conducted their own rocket mail experiments. In the 1950s, India even attempted to use rockets for mail delivery during a festival, showcasing the enduring fascination with the concept.

While rocket mail ultimately didn't revolutionize mail delivery as envisioned, it left a mark on the history of technology and communication. The daring experiments of visionaries like Schmiedl paved the way for the exploration of space and the development of more advanced rockets.

## A TASTE OF POMPEII

In the year 79 AD, the mighty Mount Vesuvius, a volcano situated near the city of Pompeii, erupted with unimaginable fury. This eruption spewed forth a massive column of ash, pumice, and rocks that blotted out the sun and rained destruction upon Pompeii. In a matter of hours, the city was buried beneath layers of volcanic debris, sealing its fate for nearly two millennia.

Pompeii, once a bustling hub of commerce and culture, was suddenly silenced. Its streets, homes, theaters, and markets vanished from the world's knowledge. But in an incredible twist of fate, this disaster preserved the city in a unique way. As centuries passed, Pompeii became a time capsule, capturing everyday life as it was in ancient Rome.

The modern rediscovery of Pompeii began in the 18th century, when excavation efforts revealed the remarkably preserved remains of this lost city. Archaeologists carefully peeled back layers of ash and dirt to unveil a world frozen in time. What they uncovered was a treasure trove of insights into Roman life – a snapshot of Pompeii's inhabitants and their customs.

Walking through Pompeii's streets today is like stepping back into the past. You can walk along the ancient stone roads, explore the ruins of lavish villas, and marvel at the colorful frescoes that adorned their walls. The city's amphitheater, where gladiators once battled, still stands as a testament to the grandeur of Roman entertainment.

One of the most captivating aspects of Pompeii's rediscovery is the plaster casts of its inhabitants. As ash covered the city, it filled every nook and cranny, including voids left by the decaying bodies of those who perished. Archaeologists developed a technique to fill these voids with plaster, creating hauntingly lifelike forms of the people who called Pompeii home.

With these plaster casts, you can see people in their final moments – crouched in fear, trying to shield themselves, or even cradling loved ones. Each cast is a silent witness to the tragedy that unfolded on that fateful day.

## THE VOYNICH MANUSCRIPT

Imagine stumbling upon a manuscript filled with strange, cryptic writing and bizarre illustrations that defy explanation. Welcome to the mysterious world of the Voynich Manuscript, a puzzle that has intrigued scholars, codebreakers, and history enthusiasts for centuries.

In the early 20th century, a rare book dealer named Wilfrid Voynich acquired a manuscript unlike any he had ever seen. Written on vellum, a type of parchment made from animal skin, the book contained a language that no one could decipher. Its 240 pages were adorned with intricate drawings of fantastical plants and mysterious symbols.

Named after its discoverer, the Voynich Manuscript became the center of attention among linguists and historians. Despite numerous attempts to crack its code, the manuscript has remained shrouded in mystery, earning it the title of "the most mysterious manuscript in the world."

The text within the Voynich Manuscript is written in an entirely unknown script. The characters are unlike any known alphabet, language, or writing system. While some have suggested that the manuscript is an elaborate hoax, its intricate details and consistent patterns have convinced many that it holds a deeper message.

The illustrations within the manuscript are equally puzzling. The botanical drawings resemble plants and herbs that defy identification, with strange combinations of leaves, stems, and roots. The human figures depicted appear otherworldly, and the celestial charts remain indecipherable. These illustrations have sparked countless theories about the origins and purpose of the manuscript.

Some believe that the Voynich Manuscript could be a lost language or a secret code, while others speculate that it may hold alchemical, religious, or herbal knowledge. Despite the dedication of countless experts, including codebreakers and linguists, the manuscript's secrets remain elusive.

As technology has advanced, the quest to unravel the Voynich Manuscript's secrets has continued. Modern techniques such as computer analysis and artificial intelligence have been applied to decode its writing and symbolism. Some progress has been made, but the manuscript's ultimate message remains tantalizingly out of reach.

The Voynich Manuscript continues to captivate minds around the world. Its pages remind us that there are still secrets to be uncovered in the vast expanse of history and that the past holds treasures that challenge our understanding and expand our horizons.

# MAKING OF THE OXFORD ENGLISH DICTIONARY

The OED (Oxford English Dictionary) is no ordinary dictionary. It's a massive compilation of words, their meanings, histories, and usage over time. But how does this incredible feat come together? The process starts with lexicographers—language experts—who meticulously gather words from a wide variety of sources, including books, magazines, websites, and more.

The journey of a word from everyday language to the OED is a journey through time. Lexicographers trace the word's origins, meanings, and changes in usage over centuries. They document its earliest appearances in written records, tracking its evolution as it gains new meanings or fades from common use.

One of the most important aspects of the OED is its focus on quotations. Lexicographers collect actual examples of how a word has been used throughout history. These quotations provide evidence of a word's usage and help define its various meanings. The OED team scours texts from different time periods, genres, and regions to create a comprehensive record.

The creation of the Oxford English Dictionary is no small task. It takes years of research, collaboration, and dedication. Lexicographers work together to draft and revise definitions, ensuring accuracy and clarity. The process involves debates, discussions, and meticulous attention to detail.

Technology has revolutionized the production of the OED. Digital tools and databases make it easier to search and analyze vast amounts of text. However, the heart of the OED remains its focus on the richness and diversity of the English language.

Once completed, the OED is published in various formats, from traditional print to digital editions. It serves as a treasure trove for language enthusiasts, scholars, writers, and anyone curious about the intricacies of words.

## THE ROTATING BUILDING

The Indiana Bell Building, also known as the "Rotating House of Telephony," was designed by architect Kurt Vonnegut Sr. Completed in 1930, this masterpiece stood 320 feet tall and served as the headquarters for the Indiana Bell Telephone Company.

When plans for a new building were made, the company initially intended to demolish the building. But then, they came up with a different idea. Why not simply *move* the building slightly to make space for more construction?

Over thirty-four days, the 11,000-ton building was slowly and carefully shifted, at a rate of 40 centimeters per hour, until it had been turned at a 90-degree angle and moved 52 feet to the side. It was an incredible, almost unbelievable, feat of modern engineering, so much so that people in the neighborhood would later say that they did not even notice the building was moving!

First, the building was essentially lifted onto rollers which were then ever so slowly rolled into position, over the five weeks it took to carry out the change. In all that time, business in the building went on as usual, with people coming in and out and conducting their business from within all day long.

Unfortunately, only thirty years later, the building was demolished to make room for new, bigger office facilities. But it has made its mark on history by being the very first building ever to be displaced, instead of being demolished.

## THE ROSE BOWL PRANK

The Rose Bowl, the college version of the Super Bowl, has seen its fair share of unforgettable moments. Yet, one event during the halftime show of the 1961 Rose Bowl between the Minnesota Golden Gophers and the Washington Huskies has etched itself into history.

Caltech, a nearby college, had always been overlooked when it came to the Rose Bowl's festivities. A group of fourteen Caltech students decided it was time to change that. Their mission? To pull off the greatest halftime prank ever seen.

While the Washington cheerleaders were away at Disneyland, a few Caltech students sneaked into their hotel rooms and found the instruction sheets for the game's flip card show - a classic method of creating images in a stadium, where students held up colored cards to form pictures. They took one as a guide and made copies, then carefully altered each instruction sheet by hand. Three of them sneaked back into the cheerleaders' hotel room to switch the original instructions with their modified ones.

Game day arrived. The Washington Huskies were leading 17-0 at halftime, and the marching band began the flip card show. The first few images went off without a hitch. But soon, the modified images emerged. One looked like a deformed husky with round ears and buck teeth, and another spelled "SEIKSUH" instead of "HUSKIES." The crowd was perplexed.

Then came the fourteenth image, displaying a single word: "CALTECH." Laughter erupted as the band left the field, and the football teams resumed play. Washington won 17-7, but the prank orchestrated by the "Fiendish Fourteen" became the stuff of legend.

## THE JOCKEY WHO CAME BACK TO LIFE

In the dramatic world of horse racing, there's a tale that defies belief. Meet Ralph Neves, a fearless jockey known as "the Portuguese Pepperpot." In 1936, at the Bay Meadows Racecourse near San Francisco, Neves found himself in a race for fame and a grand prize: $500 in cash and a gold watch.

Neves, only nineteen at the time, was on his trusty steed, Fannikins. As they sped around the track, suddenly, one of the horses in front of them stumbled, bringing four steeds crashing down. Fannikins tried to halt but tripped, throwing Neves off him.

Neves' lifeless body was moved to the track's first aid room, and the crowd fell silent upon hearing the news that he had died. However, Neves had other plans.

Dr. Horace Stevens arrived on the premises determined to save his comrade. He delivered a shot of adrenaline directly into Neves' heart. Initially, there was no response, and Dr. Stevens left, disheartened. But then, a miracle unfolded.

Roughly twenty minutes later, Neves sat up on the table, seemingly back from the dead. Half-naked, bloodied, and with a toe tag, Neves made his way to the hospital. The next morning, he sneaked out of the window, still in his gown, and hailed a cab back to the racetrack.

Returning to the track, Neves resumed the race, winning the title and the watch. The San Francisco Chronicle's headline captured the unbelievable story: "Ralph Neves – Died But Lives, to Ride and Win."

# THE BRITISH COMEBACK

Imagine you're a part of a sports team, and you desperately want to win. But there's a problem – you're not very good, and your team never wins. That's exactly how the British national cycling team felt before 2008.

They were struggling to keep up with the best cyclists in the world and hadn't won the Tour de France, the world's biggest cycling event, in over 100 years. Whatever big changes they tried to make to their training or new strategies they employed, did not help. But then, their coach, Dave Brailsford, had a brilliant idea. Instead of trying to make one big change, he decided to make lots of small ones. It was like trying to solve a big puzzle by putting tiny pieces together.

First, they changed the shape and materials of the bikes to make them sleeker and more efficient. Then, they improved the way the riders trained and made sure they ate healthy food. Another small piece of the puzzle.

They didn't focus on the big things, but on the smallest, seemingly inconsequential things as well – like making their pillows and mattresses more comfortable to help the riders sleep better, and painting the inside of their van white to better see and clean any dust that might affect their equipment.

The British cycling team didn't become champions overnight. It took time and patience. They kept working on these little changes every day. And in the 2008 Beijing Olympics, they won 8 out of 10 gold medals in cycling. They also set new world records, an unbelievable feat for the once-mediocre team.

Sometimes, it's the small, everyday things that add up to something amazing. No one could believe that changing the team's pillows or teaching the riders how best to wash their hands to avoid infections would have such a huge impact, but there you go.

# THE LIGHTNING PITCHER

Ray Caldwell had a natural talent for baseball, particularly for pitching. This skill eventually led him to the major leagues, where he played for several teams, including the New York Yankees and the Boston Red Sox.

But it was on August 24, 1919, while playing for the Cleveland Indians, that Caldwell's life took a dramatic turn. The Indians were facing the Philadelphia Athletics, and Caldwell was pitching.

As they played, storm clouds gathered overhead, and lightning cracked across the sky. Ray Caldwell was suddenly knocked to the ground, struck by lightning, and many believed he was dead.

Miraculously, after a few minutes, Caldwell got up, brushed off the dirt, and declared that he was ready to continue pitching. Remarkably, Caldwell went on to finish the game. He pitched the final out and secured a 2-1 victory for the Indians. It was an astonishing display of determination and courage, and the fans in the stadium cheered him on with admiration.

Ray Caldwell's story quickly became legendary in the world of baseball. He was known as the "lightning strike pitcher," and his incredible comeback inspired countless people. He continued to play baseball professionally for several more years, always grateful for the astounding recovery he made from a near-death experience.

# AN OLYMPIC HOCKEY MIRACLE

In the winter of 1980, the world witnessed one of the greatest underdog stories in sports history. The U.S. Olympic hockey team, made up of young, amateur players, faced off against the mighty Soviet Union team at the Winter Olympics in New York. This event would become known as the "Miracle on Ice."

The Soviet Union had a team of experienced professionals, while the U.S. team consisted of college students and a few young players from the minor leagues. Nobody expected the American team to stand a chance against the Soviets.

The game took place on February 22, 1980, and the atmosphere in the arena was electric as Team USA took the ice. The Soviet team took an early lead with a goal. But the U.S. team fought back, and by the end of the first period, the score was tied. The Americans were holding their own against the seemingly unbeatable Soviet machine.

The tension in the arena continued to build. The American players gave everything they had, blocking shots, checking their opponents, and showing incredible resilience.

Then, in the third period, with just minutes left on the clock and both teams tied with 3 points each, the U.S. team saw an opportunity. Maneuvering elegantly, they shot the puck into the goal — earning them the lead, for the first time in the game. When the final buzzer sounded, the U.S. had won.

The U.S. team went on to win the gold medal by defeating Finland in their final game, and their victory in Lake Placid remains one of the most iconic moments in Olympic history.

## AMAZING WILMA RUDOLPH

Born prematurely on June 23, 1940, in St. Bethlehem, Tennessee, Wilma Rudolph faced a challenging start to life. Stricken by illnesses, including pneumonia and scarlet fever, as well as the debilitating polio virus at the age of four, Wilma's early years were filled with hardship.

Polio left Wilma with a paralyzed left leg, making it difficult for her to walk. However, Wilma's mother, Blanche, was her unwavering source of support and encouragement. She took her daughter to physical therapy sessions several times a week, where Wilma worked tirelessly to regain her strength and mobility. This determination paid off when, at the age of nine, Wilma was finally able to walk without the need for a leg brace.

Wilma joined her high school track team at Burt High School in Clarksville, Tennessee. Her speed quickly caught the attention of her coach, who saw immense potential in Wilma and invited her to join his summer training program.

Wilma flourished in the program. Her remarkable speed and dedication allowed her to compete against top athletes and, by the age of 16, she had earned a spot on the U.S. Olympic track and field team, competing in the 1956 Melbourne Olympics.

Four years later, at the 1960 Rome Olympics, Wilma Rudolph competed in the 100-meter, 200-meter, and 4x100-meter relay events. She sprinted her way to three gold medals, becoming the first American woman to achieve such a feat in a single Olympics.

## INSPIRING YUSRA MARDINI

Yusra Mardini grew up in Damascus, Syria, dreaming of becoming an Olympic swimmer. However, her dream crumbled in 2015 when conflict and violence in Syria forced her family to flee their home. Yusra, her sister Sarah, and their parents embarked on a perilous journey to a brighter future in Europe.

Their treacherous voyage involved crossing the Aegean Sea from Turkey to Greece in a small inflatable boat. Yusra's dreams of swimming in the Olympics soon transformed into a life-saving mission. When their fragile boat's engine failed, leaving them adrift in open waters, Yusra, her sister, and two others took it upon themselves to swim behind the boat and push it forward for three hours until they reached the Greek island of Lesbos.

Their bravery and determination saved the lives of everyone on board. The family continued their journey through Europe, eventually settling in Germany, where they sought refuge.

Despite the challenges of adapting to a new country and culture, Yusra's passion for swimming and her remarkable work ethic set her on a path to achieving her Olympic dreams.

Yusra's journey culminated at the 2016 Rio Olympics, where she competed as part of the Refugee Olympic Team. Although she didn't win a medal, Yusra's participation in the Olympics was a triumph in itself. Her presence on the world stage sent a powerful message to millions of people, especially refugees and displaced individuals.

Beyond her Olympic journey, Yusra Mardini has become an advocate for refugees' rights and an ambassador for the United Nations High Commissioner for Refugees (UNHCR). She uses her platform to raise awareness about the global refugee crisis and inspire others to take action.

## FOGGY SOCCER

It was December 25, 1937, Christmas Day, when Sam Bartram's Charlton Athletic soccer team played Chelsea in a match at The Valley, Charlton's home stadium in London. The weather that day was far from ideal, with dense fog enveloping the field.

As the match began, the fog gradually thickened. Soon, the players and the ball disappeared completely from view. But the referee, relying on his whistle and the crowd's shouts, decided to let the game continue. The players had no choice but to play on, even though they could hardly see each other, or the ball they were meant to be maneuvering.

As Charlton's goalkeeper, Sam Bartram found himself in a peculiar and lonely situation. He could barely make out the faint silhouettes of his own teammates, let alone the opposing players. With each passing minute, the fog grew thicker, and the stadium became eerily quiet.

Unbeknownst to Bartram, the game had ended. Both teams had stopped playing, but no one had informed Bartram.

It wasn't until Bartram heard a distant voice shouting, "Sam, come back! They've stopped playing!" that he finally realized the truth. He had been guarding an empty field for a full 15 minutes.

Sam later said that he had been so worried about letting a goal in that he was afraid to leave the goal and see what was happening, so he just stood there, believing someone would tell him if the game ended.

The match ended in a 1-0 victory for Charlton Athletic, but the true victory belonged to Sam Bartram and his unwitting solo performance.

## FREE SOLO CLIMBER

Alex Honnold was born in Sacramento, California, in 1985. As a young boy, he was drawn to climbing, and by the age of 10, he was already scaling the walls of his local climbing gym. His passion for climbing only grew stronger over the years.

What sets Alex apart from other climbers is his dedication to "free soloing." This means he climbs without ropes or any safety equipment at all. It's just him, the rock, and the void beneath him. For most people, this would be terrifying, but for Alex, it's exhilarating.

Alex's most famous climb was El Capitan in Yosemite National Park. This colossal wall rises nearly 3,000 feet from the valley floor. In 2017, he became the first person ever to free solo El Capitan, a feat many thought was impossible. The climb took him just under four hours, with every little slip or mistake carrying life-or-death consequences.

While Alex may make it look easy, he is incredibly disciplined and cautious. He spends months, sometimes years, studying his climbs, practicing the moves, and inspecting every inch of the rock. His meticulous preparation helps minimize the risk.

While his solo climbs may be the stuff of legend, Alex's humble and down-to-earth personality has made him a role model for aspiring climbers and adventurers everywhere.

**EXTREME EXPLORATIONS**

## THE FALLING FLIGHT ATTENDANT

On a fateful winter day in January 1972, the path of Vesna Vu-lovic, a 22-year-old flight attendant, took a dramatically unex-pected turn. An administrative mix-up had placed her aboard a DC-9 airplane cruising over Czechoslovakia (now Czech Republic), instead of a different flight she was actually supposed to be on.

As the airplane soared over the picturesque landscapes, Vesna embraced the opportunity for an adventure. However, unbe-knownst to her, a terrorist group known as Ustashe had planted an explosive onboard her flight.

While the plane soared over Srbska-Kamenice, the explosive device detonated, tearing the DC-9 into fragments. The horrify-ing wreckage, along with its 28 passengers, plummeted through the sky for three agonizing minutes before crashing into a frozen mountainside.

The aftermath was a scene of devastation which no one should have survived. But rescuers arrived to discover that, against all odds, Vesna was alive. Thanks to the efforts of a first responder with wartime medical experience, Vesna re-ceived initial aid until more help could arrive.

Despite her critical condition, and contrary to medical pre-dictions, Vesna awoke from her coma just three days later. Her injuries were extensive – her skull was fractured, both her legs were broken, and her spine was crushed. Yet, by September, Vesna was fully recovered and already back at work – on the ground this time. In spite of the trauma of the fall, Vesna could not remember anything about the incident or the weeks following, and luckily for her, does not even suffer from a fear of flying.

Vesna's incredible survival has etched her name into the record books, earning her the Guinness World Record for the highest fall survived without a parachute.

# PIONEER 10

In the grand tapestry of space exploration, one silent traveler emerges as an emblem of human curiosity and ambition: NASA's Pioneer 10 space probe. Launched into the cosmos in 1973, this intrepid spacecraft has traversed a staggering thirteen billion miles, venturing through the Kuiper Belt – a realm of asteroids and comets.

Amidst its awe-inspiring journey, Pioneer 10 carries an artifact of profound significance – a 6 by 9-inch gold anodized plaque affixed to its frame. Crafted with meticulous attention, this engraving serves as a universal message, a glimpse of humanity for any intelligent beings who may encounter it. The design, etched with simple line diagrams, conveys a wealth of data about Earth and its inhabitants.

The plaque depicts a man and a woman. The man's raised right hand extends a symbol of goodwill, hopefully transcending language barriers and cultural divides. The plaque also provides a map of our solar system, highlighting our sun's position in relation to celestial markers that could enable these beings to calculate the probe's origin.

Some have speculated about the potential risks of disclosing Earth's location, fearing it could attract hostile entities. However, the sheer odds and vast timeframes involved render such concerns largely hypothetical.

In reality, the prospect of Pioneer 10 or its sibling probe, Pioneer 11, encountering intelligent life is exceedingly remote. Yet, this endeavor is fueled by the pure optimism inherent to humanity's exploration spirit. The message, carved in gold and etched in the tapestry of space, speaks of our desire to share a glimpse of ourselves with the cosmos.

As Pioneer 10 voyages through the cosmic sea, its faint radio whispers grow dimmer. Yet, with each passing moment, this silent traveler carries forth the unspoken hopes and aspirations of Earth, a beacon of our species' indomitable spirit venturing into the infinite expanse beyond our world.

# THE BERMUDA TRIANGLE

Few mysteries are as bemusing as the mystery of the Bermuda Triangle. Nestled between the points of Florida, Bermuda, and Puerto Rico, this enigmatic expanse of ocean has baffled scientists and adventurers alike. The Bermuda Triangle, also known as the Devil's Triangle, has become synonymous with tales of disappearances and unexplained phenomena. Countless ships and airplanes have seemingly vanished within its bounds, sparking theories ranging from the plausible to the fantastical. But what exactly makes this area so special?

One of the most intriguing aspects of the Bermuda Triangle is the sudden and unexplained disappearances of ships and aircraft. Some of the most famous cases include Flight 19, a group of five U.S. Navy bombers that vanished in 1945 during a training flight, and the cargo ship USS Cyclops, which disappeared in 1918 with 306 people aboard, never to be seen again. These incidents have fueled speculation about everything from alien abductions to time warps.

Researchers have explored various theories to explain the Bermuda Triangle's mysteries. Some scientists suggest that natural factors, such as unpredictable weather patterns, strong ocean currents, and magnetic anomalies, could contribute to navigational errors and accidents. Others propose that methane gas trapped beneath the seafloor could create bubbles that disrupt buoyancy and lead to sudden sinkings.

Despite the allure of supernatural explanations, experts emphasize that the Bermuda Triangle's disappearance rate is not significantly higher than in other parts of the world. In fact, many incidents can be attributed to human error, technical malfunctions, and even piracy.

The Bermuda Triangle's mysteries continue to capture the imagination, inspiring countless books, documentaries, and movies. While the true nature of the phenomena remains open to debate, it serves as a reminder that the vast oceans hold secrets that we are still struggling to understand.

## POLAR EXPLORATION

Roald Amundsen, a Norwegian explorer born in 1872, was a man of determination and vision. His dream was to conquer the earth's most remote and challenging places—the North and South Poles, which had yet to be explored. With meticulous planning and an unyielding spirit, Amundsen set out to achieve what many considered impossible.

In 1903, Amundsen embarked on his first major expedition, leading a crew aboard his ship, the Gjøa, to navigate the treacherous Northwest Passage. This challenging waterway connected the Atlantic and Pacific Oceans through the Arctic Ocean. For three years, Amundsen and his team faced extreme cold, navigational challenges, and encounters with native Inuit communities. Through their sheer determination, they successfully completed the passage in 1906, marking a historic achievement.

However, it was Amundsen's conquest of the *South* Pole that put his name in the history books of exploration. In 1911, he set out with a team on an exhausting journey across Antarctica. Through freezing temperatures, blizzards, and treacherous terrain, they reached the South Pole on December 14, 1911, becoming the first humans to stand at the southernmost point of the earth.

Amundsen and his team relied on sled dogs and skis for transportation, and their careful preparation ensured they had adequate supplies and clothing for the grueling journey. This focus on practicality and innovation set Amundsen apart as a true leader in exploration.

As remarkable as his achievements were, Amundsen's humility and respect for the regions he explored also stood out. He learned from local indigenous people, adopted their clothing and techniques, and forged strong connections with the communities he encountered.

Amundsen's legacy continued with his groundbreaking flight over the North Pole in 1926 and his explorations on the airship Norge in 1928. Tragically, in 1928, while attempting a rescue mission for an Italian explorer, Amundsen's plane disappeared over the Arctic Ocean, and he was never seen again.

## LAIKA THE SPACE DOG

Amidst the Cold War rivalry between the Soviet Union and the United States, the Soviet space program sought to demonstrate its capabilities by launching living organisms into space. Laika, a stray dog, was chosen for the mission. On November 3, 1957, Sputnik 2 lifted off with Laika on board, becoming the first living creature to orbit Earth.

However, the mission was fraught with ethical controversy. Laika's fate was sealed; the technology of the time did not allow for her return to Earth. Her mission was essentially a one-way trip, and the decision to send a living being into space without a return plan ignited debates on the morality of such endeavors.

Laika's journey provided valuable insights into the effects of space travel on living organisms. Data collected during her mission contributed to our understanding of how weightlessness and space conditions impact physiological functions. Her sacrifice paved the way for advancements in human spaceflight by highlighting potential challenges and risks.

The scientific community recognized the limitations and shortcomings of Laika's mission. The ordeal sparked discussions about animal welfare, prompting changes in how animals are treated in scientific research. The ethical dilemmas surrounding Laika's mission prompted a reevaluation of the responsibilities that come with pushing the boundaries of scientific exploration.

Today, Laika's story serves as a reminder of the early days of space exploration, characterized by ambition and the pursuit of scientific knowledge. Her legacy endures in the broader context of humanity's achievements in conquering the challenges of space travel. Her mission, controversial as it may have been, remains a milestone in our journey to understand and explore the cosmos.

## 127 HOURS

In April 2003, Aron Ralston, an experienced outdoorsman and avid climber, set out on a solo canyoneering adventure in Blue John Canyon, Utah. He was well-prepared, with climbing gear, food, and water. However, what was meant to be a routine adventure quickly turned into a nightmare.

While exploring the narrow canyons, a massive boulder, weighing over 800 pounds, became dislodged and trapped Aron's right arm against the canyon wall. He was unable to move or free himself, and he soon realized the severity of his situation. He was trapped in a remote location with no cell phone signal and he hadn't told anyone where he was.

For 127 hours, over five days, Aron rationed his meager food and water supply and tried to chip away at the boulder using a cheap multitool. He waited and waited for someone to rescue him, but though his loved ones knew he was missing, they had no way of finding him in the vast canyon.

With no hope of rescue in sight and facing the real possibility of death, Aron made the agonizing decision to amputate his trapped arm. Bracing himself, he first broke the bones in his arm. Then, using a dull blade, he cut through the remaining tissue and tendons, finally freeing himself.

Afterward, he rappelled down the canyon walls and encountered a family who provided him with much-needed assistance and alerted authorities. He was rescued and rushed to the hospital, where he received medical attention and began his long road to recovery. The movie "127 Hours" captures his remarkable journey.

## THE DYATLOV PASS INCIDENT

In the winter of 1959, a group of experienced hikers embarked on a trek through the Ural Mountains in Russia. They were led by Igor Dyatlov, a seasoned outdoorsman. However, what was supposed to be an adventurous journey turned into one of the most perplexing mysteries in history — the Dyatlov Pass Incident.

The hikers, mostly students from the Ural Polytechnic Institute, set out on their expedition in late January. Their goal was to reach Otorten Mountain, located in a remote and challenging terrain. The group was well-prepared, carrying essential supplies, warm clothing, and tents.

As the days passed, the group's progress was monitored through diary entries and photographs. But when the expedition's expected return date came and went without any word from them, their families grew concerned. A rescue mission was organized, and searchers soon made a chilling discovery.

The searchers found the group's abandoned and badly damaged tent on the slopes of Kholat Syakhl, which translates to "Dead Mountain." The tent had been slashed from the inside, and all the group's belongings were left behind, including their shoes and warm clothing.

As they followed tracks in the snow, the searchers found the first two bodies. They were shoeless and dressed only in their underwear, despite the freezing temperatures. Three more bodies were found near a makeshift campfire, seemingly trying to stay warm. The last four hikers were found in a ravine, injured and buried under several feet of snow. Yet, there were no external signs of a struggle or any clear evidence of an attacker.

To this day, the Dyatlov Pass Incident remains unsolved. No one has even the slightest idea of what happened to these young, talented hikers on their last harrowing journey.

## POOP COFFEE

Kopi Luwak coffee, often referred to as "civet coffee," is known for its distinct flavor and rarity, but more so, for its interesting – some would even say disgusting – method of production. The production process begins with the civet, a small mammal that lives in the coffee-growing regions of Indonesia, the Philippines, and other parts of Asia. These furry creatures have a taste for ripe coffee cherries, which they consume hungrily.

After the civet eats the cherries, the coffee beans pass through its digestive system. Enzymes in the civet's stomach alter the beans' composition and flavor profile. Then, the civet poops – and out come the coffee beans. The digested beans are then collected from the civet's droppings, thoroughly cleaned, and processed.

This unique fermentation process is thought to contribute to the coffee's smooth and distinct flavor. The beans' exposure to the civet's digestive enzymes can reduce their bitterness and acidity while enhancing their earthy and chocolaty undertones.

After being collected, the beans are roasted and ground, just like any other coffee beans. The result is a cup of Kopi Luwak coffee that offers a unique blend of flavors and aromas, different from your typical cup of joe.

# THE VOLCANO ISLAND

In 1963, a series of underwater eruptions began just off the coast of Iceland. The eruptions, caused by volcanic activity beneath the sea floor, released tremendous amounts of heat and energy. As molten lava met the cold waters of the North Atlantic, an awe-inspiring transformation began.

Over the course of a few weeks, the intense heat caused the surrounding seawater to boil and evaporate, resulting in massive explosions. The explosions threw ash, steam, and rocks high into the air, creating a spectacular volcanic display visible from miles away. As the eruptions continued, a brand-new island began to form.

The island, named Surtsey after a Norse fire giant, emerged as a result of this dramatic volcanic activity. Lava flows and ash accumulated, gradually forming a landmass that broke through the ocean's surface. Surtsey's birth was an event witnessed by scientists and researchers who were fortunate enough to observe this incredible process in real time.

Surtsey provided scientists with a unique opportunity to study the formation of new land and the colonization of life. As the island cooled and solidified, plants and animals began to make their way to this fresh terrain. Birds, insects, and even seals arrived, marking the beginning of an ecological colonization that demonstrated the resilience of life even in the harshest environments.

Earth is a dynamic and ever-changing realm, where natural forces continue to reshape the land and constantly create new opportunities for life to flourish.

# THE TUNGUSKA EVENT

In the early morning of June 30, 1908, deep in the Siberian wilderness near the Tunguska River, a colossal explosion was suddenly heard. This event, known as the Tunguska Event, remains one of the most perplexing and mysterious incidents in scientific history.

The explosion flattened around 800 square miles of the surrounding forest, an area bigger than the whole of New York City. Around 80 million trees were burned and knocked over, creating a circular pattern around the center of the explosion. The closest eyewitnesses, who were hundreds of miles away, reported seeing the sky bright and glowing despite the early hour. Over the next few days, the sky stayed aglow. The shockwave from the explosion could be felt as far away as England!

From the very first day, the cause of the explosion was a complete mystery to the world. For decades, scientists puzzled over what could have caused the massive event. Various theories emerged, but none were able to provide a definitive explanation. Then, once it was deemed safe, expeditions began to reach the remote region to explore, and uncovered some interesting clues.

One leading theory is that a meteor or comet, composed of ice and rock, entered Earth's atmosphere and disintegrated before reaching the surface. Researchers at the site found elevated levels of iridium, a chemical element that is rare on Earth but sometimes found in bodies from outer space.

We might never know what exactly caused the 1908 Tunguska event, and we can only hope that if something similar does happen in the future, we can be better prepared.

## WATERMELON SNOW

If you were to take a hike through snowy mountains, you might come across an interesting phenomenon – a blanket of reddish-pink snow also known as "watermelon snow."

Watermelon snow, also called "snow algae," is a peculiar occurrence that transforms the snowy landscape into shades of pink or red during the summer months. But what causes this phenomenon?

Watermelon snow gets its unique color from microscopic algae called Chlamydomonas nivalis. These single-celled organisms love cold, high-altitude environments best, and when they accumulate in large numbers, despite how small they are, they are numerous enough to create a vibrant pink or red hue directly beneath the snow.

Then, when the weather starts to get warmer, the snow begins to melt, revealing the colorful snow beneath. Even Charles Darwin made note of this captivating phenomenon during his explorations.

The question that crosses most minds upon encountering the magical watermelon snow is – Is it safe to eat?? While the algae themselves are not toxic, consuming large quantities of pink snow is not recommended. In fact, eating a lot of regular snow is not such a good idea either, because it can absorb dirt and bacteria from its surroundings.

So, the next time you see a patch of pink or red snow at the beginning of spring, you'll know that it's not just a visual spectacle or someone having fun with red dye. It's cool scientific evidence of just how amazing nature really is.

## THE RED RAIN OF KERALA

On July 25, 2001 in Kerala, India, people woke up to a strange and unsettling sight that must have seemed like something straight out of a sci-fi movie. It was raining, as it often does in the area, but instead of clear, watery droplets – it seemed to be raining blood.

The rain that was falling from the sky was deep red in color and ran over the ground in red streams. Once the initial shock and fear had subsided, scientists got straight to work collecting samples of the mysterious liquid. Initial tests revealed the presence of microscopic particles in the water, but their origin was unclear.

One of the most astonishing theories proposed was that the red rain might contain actual extraterrestrial life forms. Some scientists believed that these particles could be alien microbes brought to Earth on a comet or meteorite. Of course, this theory sparked global curiosity.

But soon, subsequent studies proved that the red particles were not aliens but terrestrial life forms. They were identified as a type of algae called Trentepohlia annulate, which was lifted into the atmosphere by powerful drafts and then traveled to Kerala and released in the red rain.

The red rain phenomenon actually returned once again in 2012, leading scientists to further investigate its causes. While the exact mechanisms behind this event remain uncertain, it's believed to be connected to atmospheric and meteorological factors.

## FIRE RAINBOWS

Rainbows are a magical, beautiful meteorological event caused when light hits a water droplet and then reflects off the inside of the droplet. Rainbows everywhere make people stop and stare, marveling at the beauty of nature.

But when the exact right conditions occur, an even more stunning phenomenon can be observed – the fire rainbow.

Fire rainbows are not technically rainbows. They are caused not by the co-occurrence of water droplets and direct sunlight, but by sunlight passing through high clouds filled with tiny ice crystals. When the sunlight hits the crystals it disperses through the air, causing a bright explosion of vibrant colors against the cloud.

Unlike regular rainbows which create a perfect circle with the sun at their center, fire rainbows are suspended in the air and do not assume an arc shape. They are also visible for a shorter time, usually no longer than a few minutes, and are far more rare, due to the very specific conditions needed for them to form. The sun has to be elevated at least 58 degrees in the sky, which means that fire rainbows are mostly observed in the afternoon. Also, the clouds have to be just the right type (cirrus clouds with hexagonal ice crystals) and the crystals have to be organized in a certain pattern.

These fiery celestial visions are as beautiful as they are rare, making them one of the most intriguing and captivating natural phenomena in our world.

# THE ABRAHAM LAKE
# FROZEN AIR BUBBLES

Imagine walking across a frozen lake, the ice beneath your feet so clear you can see right through it. Below, instead of the calm, clear water of the lake, your eyes detect thousands of little air bubbles trapped in icy cages, creating a breathtaking sight. This remarkable winter magic phenomenon happens exclusively at Abraham Lake in Alberta.

Abraham Lake is not a natural lake but a reservoir formed by the Bighorn Dam on the North Saskatchewan River in Alberta, Canada. The lake stretches over 20 miles and is a popular visiting destination throughout the year.

What makes the lake truly exceptional is what happens beneath its icy surface during the winter. When temperatures plummet and the lake's surface freezes, methane gas, produced by the decomposition of organic matter in the lakebed, gets trapped under the ice. This gas shifts and forms intricate patterns as it rises toward the surface.

These methane bubbles gradually make their way toward the ice ceiling, getting bigger and bigger. As they rise closer to the cold surface, they begin to freeze, eventually capturing the gas bubble as it is suspended in the water. As more and more ice bubbles rise and freeze, the result is a stunning, frozen underwater gallery, with bubbles of every size.

Abraham Lake's frozen air bubbles have become a magnet for photographers seeking to capture their beauty. Every winter, the lake attracts visitors from around the world who come to witness and photograph this remarkable phenomenon.

# POLAND'S CROOKED FOREST

In a remote corner of western Poland, a peculiar grove of pine trees known as the "Crooked Forest" stands out. This interesting collection of trees has puzzled scientists and intrigued nature enthusiasts for decades, and its mysteries continue to baffle all who encounter it.

The small Crooked Forest is nestled within the larger Gryfino Forest, near the town of Gryfino in western Poland. What makes this forest so distinctive is the unusual shape its trees grow. About 400 pine trees in the Crooked Forest bend at a 90-degree angle just near their base, causing them to grow in a sharp curve sideways before eventually straightening upward again. The phenomenon is especially striking because it affects nearly all the trees in this small forest!

The origins of the Crooked Forest's unique trees are debated among scientists and experts. One prominent theory suggests that during their formative years, perhaps in the 1930s or 1940s, the trees were deliberately manipulated by human hands. Some speculate that the bend was created for furniture or boat production. However, no concrete evidence has emerged to confirm this hypothesis.

Another theory proposes that heavy snowfall during the trees' early growth years caused them to bend under the weight. Alternatively, some suggest that a unique combination of wind patterns and gravitational forces influenced the trees' growth. Unfortunately, none of these theories provide a definitive explanation for the forest's distinct curvature.

Despite the mystery surrounding their origin, the Crooked Forest's trees are very much alive and continue to grow. Over the years, their trunks have thickened and branches have extended, but they still remain confusingly crooked, even after all these years.

## A DWARF AND A GIANT

The human body is a remarkable system, capable of extraordinary feats. Adam Rainer, born in Graz, Austria, in 1899, is a unique and extraordinary case of the extremes of human anatomy.

Adam Rainer was born with an inherited form of dwarfism, known as proportionate dwarfism. Throughout his early years, he experienced the challenges that came with being exceptionally short. At age 18, he stood at a mere 4 feet 0.25 inches tall, making him considerably shorter than his peers. Despite the widespread conscription to fight for the Austo-Hungarian army in World War I, Rainer was refused entry to the military ranks due to his size.

Then, Rainer's life took a dramatic turn when he reached adulthood. Around the age of 18, his body began to undergo an unprecedented transformation. Instead of stopping at the typical height for people with dwarfism, Rainer suddenly began to grow again.

His extreme growth spurt was nothing short of astonishing. By the age of 21, he had surpassed 7 feet in height – an unbelievable change from the shorter-than-average kid he had been until then.

Rainer's unusual growth was the result of a rare combination of medical conditions. As a child, his proportionate dwarfism had restricted his growth. However, a later condition known as acromegaly began to take effect. Acromegaly is a disorder caused by an overproduction of growth hormone in the body. In Rainer's case, it led to an extreme and uncontrolled increase in his height.

Sadly, Adam Rainer passed away in 1950 at the age of 51. His case was one of extremes – from dwarfism to towering height. He became a medical curiosity and a symbol of the remarkable and often perplexing mysteries of the human body.

# ESCAPE FROM SLAVERY

Until the 1860s, slavery in America was very common. While most people born into slavery would sadly live and die without knowing a life of freedom, Ona Judge was a unique soul who dared to escape her reality of slavery and pursue a better life.

Ona Judge was born around 1773 at Mount Vernon, the Virginia estate of George and Martha Washington. From the time she was a young child, she served as a personal maid to Martha Washington. Growing up, she toiled away, performing household chores and tending to the needs of the family.

But in May 1796, Ona Judge's life took an unexpected turn. She discovered that Martha Washington intended to give her away as a wedding gift to her granddaughter. Unable to bear the thought of living her entire life as a slave, Ona made a decision – to seize her chance and escape to freedom. On May 21, 1796, she slipped away from a mansion in Philadelphia, where the Washingtons were residing at the time.

Ona's escape plan was daring and well-executed. She sought refuge with free African Americans in Philadelphia and later in New Hampshire, moving around constantly to avoid her steps being traced. Her escape was a shock to the Washington household, and President Washington made many attempts to have her return, even offering bribes if she came back of her own will. Yet, Ona was determined to be free.

Thankfully, Ona Judge got a happy ending. She married a free black sailor named Jack Staines and the couple had three children and built a life together, living free from the bonds of slavery. Ona's remarkable journey from servitude to freedom became a symbol of resistance against the institution of slavery.

# UNPARALLELED MEMORY

When you think back on the things you've experienced in your life, you probably notice that your memory is made up of small moments and significant events. No one remembers every single second of their life or every little piece of information they've ever been told, right?

Wrong.

Brad Williams, born in 1953, possesses a rare and extraordinary ability known as hyperthymesia, or highly superior autobiographical memory (HSAM). We have two types of memory: autobiographical memory, which relates to things that we have seen, felt, and experienced, and episodic memory, which refers to specific events and pieces of information. Hyperthymesia allows Brad to remember an astonishing amount of his own life experiences with remarkable clarity.

Brad's incredible memory goes beyond just remembering important events or milestones; he can recall what he had for breakfast on a specific day years ago or describe the weather on a random date from his past. His memory is like a continuous, unbroken movie of his life, which he can recount down to the tiniest detail.

His unique memory was first recognized and documented by researchers in the early 2000s. He was part of an initial study on individuals with HSAM, which revealed the astonishing extent of his memory abilities.

While Brad's extraordinary memory can be a blessing, it can also be a challenge. He often finds himself reliving past events and experiences, both positive and negative, in vivid detail. It's as though he's constantly living in multiple moments of his life simultaneously.

Brad Williams' story of hyperthymesia sheds light on the incredible complexity of the human brain. While many of us struggle to remember even recent events, individuals like Brad have the extraordinary ability to recall their entire lives in intricate detail.

# THE WITCH POISON OF SALEM

In the late 1600s, a Puritan settlement called Salem in Massachusetts became the center of a strange and chaotic event – the Salem witch trials. It started when two young girls began to present bizarre symptoms like uncontrollable fits, screams, and strange contortions. The village doctor couldn't explain their condition, so he decreed that the girls must be witches.

Soon, others in the settlement began to exhibit similar mysterious behavior, and accusations of witchcraft began to fly.

The trials that followed led to the execution of nineteen people and the imprisonment of many more under suspicion of supernatural wrongdoing. Today, most people agree that those punished in Salem were not guilty of witchcraft, yet the true cause of their strange behavior remains a mystery. One intriguing theory suggests that the community's rye crop may have played a role, and rye may have contributed to other mysterious events in history as well.

Ryegrass, a common grain crop in Salem, can become infected with a fungus called Claviceps purpurea during its growth. This fungus produces alkaloids during its development that can cause physiological problems when ingested by humans.

Ergot poisoning, or ergotism, can lead to a range of symptoms. It usually starts with problems like nausea, diarrhea, and vomiting. Then, it affects the central nervous system, causing symptoms such as headaches, tingling sensations, itching, spasms, convulsions, unconsciousness, and hallucinations.

Historians now speculate that other strange events, like the "dancing epidemic" in Europe from the 14th to the 17th century, may have been caused by ergot poisoning. This phenomenon made groups of people dance uncontrollably through the streets, often speaking nonsense and foaming at the mouth until they collapsed from exhaustion.

While the true cause of the Salem witch trials remains a subject of debate, the influence of ergot in history, from ancient Greece to modern medicine, is undeniable.

# MISS UNSINKABLE

Violet Jessop, nicknamed "Miss Unsinkable," led a life that was nothing short of extraordinary. Born on October 2, 1887, in Argentina, she would go on to survive not one, but two major shipwrecks during the early 20th century!

Violet came from a family of Irish immigrants, and her father was a sheep farmer. When her father passed away suddenly, she began working as a stewardess.

In 1910, she got a job working for the Royal Mail Line as a stewardess on a British ocean liner, and one year later she was on board the Titanic, serving as a stewardess during its first and only voyage.

When the Titanic struck an iceberg on April 14, 1912, Violet was assigned to lifeboat 16. Miraculously, she survived the sinking and was rescued, unlike many others who drowned at sea.

Surviving the Titanic was enough excitement for one lifetime, but Violet's adventures were far from over. She continued her career as a stewardess and, in 1916, found herself on board the HMS Britannic, the Titanic's sister ship. During World War I, the Britannic had been converted into a hospital ship. Tragically, it struck a mine in the Aegean Sea. Remarkably, Violet survived yet again, escaping on another lifeboat.

Violet Jessop's remarkable ability to survive not one, but two major maritime disasters earned her the nickname "Miss Unsinkable." She passed away on May 5, 1971, but her incredible story lives on as a symbol of hope and determination.

# THE GREEN CHILDREN OF WOOLPIT

Once upon a time, in the small English village of Woolpit during the 12th century, two children, a boy and a girl, appeared suddenly as though out of thin air. What made their arrival strange was not just the unexpected nature of it — but the fact that these children's skin was completely green.

The villagers were baffled by these peculiar children. Not only did they have a greenish hue to their skin, but they also spoke a language that no one in Woolpit could understand and their clothing was unlike anything anyone had seen before.

The villagers took the children in and fed them, but sadly, the boy soon died. The girl adapted to her new surroundings and her green skin slowly began to fade.

The girl eventually lost her green complexion completely, became a part of the Woolpit community, and even got married. As she learned English, she explained that she and her brother came from a place where everything was green. She couldn't provide many details about their home, all she remembered was that everything and everyone was completely green.

Today, the story of the Green Children of Woolpit remains a famous legend. While we may never know the real truth behind their origins, their tale continues to captivate the imagination of people worldwide.

## THE SILENT TWINS

On April 11, 1963, in Wales, two extraordinary identical twins named June and Jennifer Gibbons were born.

From a young age, June and Jennifer displayed a remarkable bond. They communicated in a secret language only they could understand and often isolated themselves from the rest of the world. While they did communicate with one another, they hardly communicated with anyone else at all. They believed that speaking to others would ultimately lead to one of their deaths. This gave them the nickname "The Silent Twins."

Their isolation deepened when they were sent to separate boarding schools in an attempt to encourage their individual development. However, this only resulted in the girls becoming more withdrawn. They would spend hours writing diaries and stories in a joint fictional world they had invented, known as the "Marvis" universe.

When the twins were 18, they turned to a life of crime, engaging in vandalism and arson. Their actions led to their arrest and admittance to Broadmoor Hospital, a high-security psychiatric institution.

Over time, the twins began to write novels and poems. They would take turns writing, each continuing the other's sentences, still talking only to each other.

In March 1993, at the age of 29, Jennifer passed away unexpectedly. Her death remains a mystery, with the exact cause unknown. Her sister, June, was devastated but continued to write and express herself through her work.

## THE HUMAN LIGHTNING ROD

In the tranquil wilderness of Shenandoah National Park, a devoted park ranger named Roy Sullivan roamed the forests and mountains. But Sullivan was no ordinary ranger; he was known as the "Human Lightning Rod" for his unbelievable encounters with lightning strikes.

Sullivan's legendary story started in 1942 when he survived his first lightning strike. While on lookout duty, a bolt of lightning hit him, burning off his eyebrows and blasting him several feet away. This electrifying experience earned him a nickname and a deep-seated fear of lightning.

Remarkably, over the next few decades, Sullivan found himself struck by lightning on an additional whopping six occasions, earning him a place in the Guinness World Records as the person struck by lightning the most times. Each encounter left him with various injuries, from burned skin and singed hair to injured ankles and chest pains – but very much alive.

Scientists estimate that the odds of being struck by lightning just once in a lifetime are around 1 in 3,000,000. Yet, Sullivan endured seven strikes!

Roy's eventful life wasn't limited to lightning strikes. He also rescued a man from a burning truck, successfully fended off a bear attack with a tree branch, and even managed to outrun a furious grizzly bear while working as a ranger.

Despite his incredible run-ins with nature's fury, Roy Sullivan remained dedicated to his job as a park ranger. He retired in 1977 after 36 years of service but continued to share his story, inspiring many with his remarkable survival.

## THE FERAL CHILD

In the heart of the Indian jungle more than a century ago, a remarkable story unfolded, one that may have gone on to become the inspiration for the famous children's book, The Jungle Book. It's the tale of Dina Sanichar, a young boy who was raised by wolves and grew up far away from humans, deep in the jungle.

Dina Sanichar was discovered by hunters in the mid-19th century near a remote forest in India. The hunters were stunned when they encountered what appeared to be a wild boy, living among a pack of wolves. The child behaved more like a wolf than a human being, his skin was covered in hair, his nails were long and sharp, and he walked on all fours.

It's believed that Dina was abandoned by his parents at a very young age and somehow found his way into the care of a wolf pack. At his young age, he adapted to the habits and behaviors of the wolves, including hunting for food, imitating their howls, and living in their dens.

The hunters who discovered Dina Sanichar brought him back to civilization. It was a challenging process to teach Dina to wear clothes, use utensils, and communicate verbally. His unique experience taught researchers a lot about the adaptability of the human brain and just how important early childhood experiences are for our development.

# PIANO PRODIGY

In the history of classical music, there are stars who shine brightly, and then there is Hazel Scott—a piano prodigy whose brilliance on the keys and unyielding commitment to justice left an indelible mark on both the world of music and civil rights.

Hazel was born in 1920 in Trinidad and Tobago but grew up in New York City. She demonstrated a remarkable talent for music from a very young age. By the time she was just three years old, she was already playing the piano, and her natural gift was evident to all who heard her.

Scott's extraordinary talent opened doors for her in a world where racism often shut them. At the age of 8 she was already auditioning for Juilliard, a school with a minimum acceptance age of 16. In the 1930s, she became the first Black woman to have her own radio show, "The Hazel Scott Show." Her dazzling piano performances captured the hearts of audiences across the nation.

Scott's musical prowess led her to Hollywood, where she became a sought-after actress, starring in films like "The Heat's On" and "Rhapsody in Blue." She also continued her music career, releasing successful albums and performing on huge stages, including Carnegie Hall.

But Hazel Scott wasn't content with just entertaining audiences; she was also an advocate for civil rights. She refused to perform in segregated venues and used her platform to speak out against racial discrimination. Her bold stance often brought her into conflict with the establishment, but she remained unwavering in her commitment to justice.

Hazel Scott's dazzling talent at the piano and her unyielding commitment to equality took her far in life, and she continues to inspire generations of musicians and activists.

## MEDICAL MARVELS

### MORGELLONS DISEASE

Morgellons disease is a baffling condition where people experience a range of bizarre, unexplained symptoms, including crawling sensations on the skin, itching, and the perception of fibers emerging from their skin. While the cause remains unclear, patients often report a distressing impact on their daily lives.

Despite the vivid descriptions, the exact nature of the fibers remains a subject of debate. Some believe that the fibers are man-made or environmental in origin, while others think they could be a biological result of the body's response to the condition. These fibers, often colored and sometimes fluorescent, have sparked curiosity and skepticism alike.

Scientists and doctors have conducted extensive research to understand Morgellons disease. However, due to the lack of a clear biological cause, some medical professionals view the condition as a type of delusional disorder known as "delusional parasitosis." This term refers to the belief that you have parasites despite no evidence to support it. Basically, they believe that Morgellons disease is no more than an imagined condition with no basis in reality.

Morgellons disease showcases the ongoing challenge of understanding complex medical conditions. The condition challenges both patients and medical professionals to think critically and compassionately. The mysteries surrounding Morgellons disease remind us that the field of medicine is ever-evolving, and the quest for answers requires a combination of scientific research, open dialogue, and a commitment to improving the lives of those affected.

## THE DANCING PLAGUE

In the summer of 1518, a woman named Frau Troffea began dancing in the streets of Strasbourg, France. Soon, others joined her, and within days, around 400 people were caught up in a frenzy. They danced wildly, without rest, for hours and even days. Their actions defied explanation and went beyond ordinary dance.

The dancing was far from celebratory. Witnesses described the dancers as having pained and tormented expressions. Many participants collapsed from exhaustion, dehydration, or heart attacks. Some even danced themselves to death! The phenomenon caused alarm in the city, with authorities trying various methods to stop the dancing, including hiring musicians to play calming music and building a stage to encourage the dancers to keep moving until they collapsed.

In the end, the dancing went on from July to September, when it began to subside. The dancers who had survived were sent to a shrine in the mountains to pray for absolution.

Medical professionals of the time struggled to understand the cause of the dancing plague. Some believed it was caused by overheated blood or a type of fungus, while others attributed it to divine punishment or even possession by demons. Today, researchers speculate that the dancing plague could have been the result of psychological stress, mass hysteria, or a form of collective psychogenic disorder.

There are reports of similar events taking place in the Middle Ages, but none as excessive as the Strasbourg Dancing Plague.

# PHINEAS GAGE'S CLOSE CALL

Phineas Gage was a railroad construction foreman in Vermont, USA. On September 13, 1848, while working on a railroad project, a tragic accident occurred. An iron rod—an inch and a quarter thick and three and a half feet long—was propelled directly through Gage's head in a freak explosion. The rod entered under his left eye, passed through his brain, and exited the top of his skull.

Remarkably, Phineas Gage survived the accident, but his life was forever altered. What made his case truly extraordinary was the profound change in his personality and behavior. Prior to the accident, Gage was known as a responsible and hardworking individual. However, after the incident, he became impulsive, irritable, and socially inappropriate.

The connection between the rod's trajectory through his brain and these personality changes was a revelation in the field of neuroscience. Gage's case provided valuable evidence that specific areas of the brain are responsible for different functions, and different parts of our personality. In Gage's case, damage to the frontal lobes of his brain led to changes in how he behaved in social interactions.

Gage's story also showed the brain's remarkable capacity for adaptation. Despite enduring such a traumatic injury, after extensive surgery, he was able to relearn basic skills and continue with his life to some extent.

Phineas Gage's experience significantly contributed to our understanding of the brain's role in controlling behavior, personality, and decision-making. His story continues to be studied by neuroscientists, psychologists, and medical professionals to this day.

# THE DEADLIEST SURGEON

Robert Liston was a skilled surgeon known for his speed and efficiency in the operating room in a time when medical technology was not yet very advanced. He was a true pioneer of his time, developing new techniques and approaches to surgical procedures. However, Liston is perhaps best remembered for an unfortunate incident that led to a 300% mortality rate in one of his surgeries!

In the early 19th century, surgeries were conducted without the aid of anesthesia. Patients often suffered immense pain during procedures, making speed a crucial factor in reducing suffering. Liston's reputation for swift surgeries led to his nickname, "the fastest knife in the West End."

Unfortunately, Liston's desire for speed led to a tragic mistake during a surgery in 1847. He was performing an amputation on a patient's leg, aiming to complete the procedure as quickly as possible. In his haste, he accidentally amputated the fingers of his assistant with his surgical blade, as well.

The patient later died of complications, the assistant's wound became infected, and even a spectator in the operating theater died of shock. This series of unfortunate events resulted in a 300% mortality rate linked to just one single surgery.

Despite this tragic incident, Liston's contributions to medicine were significant. He pioneered new techniques for surgeries, advocated for the use of ether as an anesthetic, and played a role in advancing surgical education and training.

## SPLIT-BRAIN

The brain, as you may know, is divided into two hemispheres: the left and the right. These hemispheres work together to control different aspects of our body and mind. The left side of the brain generally controls the actions and sensations of the right side of the body, and vice versa. One of the only parts of the brain that is asymmetrical is the area that controls language – how we speak and understand it – which is located only on the left side of the brain. Other than that, the brain is in near-perfect symmetry. However, in some rare cases, the connection between the left and right hemispheres is disrupted, leading to a condition called split-brain phenomenon.

Split-brain syndrome usually occurs when the corpus callosum, a bundle of nerve fibers connecting the two hemispheres right along the middle of the brain, is severed. This procedure was sometimes performed in the past as a last resort to treat severe epilepsy, a neurological disorder causing seizures.

One of the most intriguing aspects of split-brain syndrome is how it affects a person's perception and behavior. Since the hemispheres can no longer directly communicate with each other, each hemisphere learns to operate independently. This means that one side of the brain might have information or experiences that the other side is not aware of.

Experiments conducted on split-brain patients revealed an extraordinary phenomenon. When an image was shown only to the *left* eye of these patients, the image was only processed by the *right* hemisphere – and not the left. When asked to describe what they saw, the patients would say that they saw nothing – because the language area of their brain, which allows them to speak, is located on the left side, which never actually saw the image!

Researchers have conducted fascinating experiments to explore the split-brain phenomenon. They've found that the left hemisphere is more dominant in processing language and logical information, while the right hemisphere excels at recognizing shapes and patterns.

## THE MAN WITH TWO FACES

Edward Mordake is said to have lived in the 19th century and was born with a peculiar anomaly—an entire second face on the back of his head, just like Professor Quirrel in the first Harry Potter book. This unusual condition is known as diprosopus, where a person is born with two faces due to the incomplete splitting of the embryo during development in the womb.

According to the legend, Mordake's extra face was even capable of grimacing, laughing, and whispering dreadful things in the dead of night—things that only Mordake could hear.

The tale of Edward Mordake has been passed down through generations. Some suggest that the story might have been embellished or even fabricated over time, blending fact and fiction into a chilling narrative, while others believe it to be undoubtedly true.

The legend of Edward Mordake endures as a captivating mystery, tapping into our fascination with the uncanny and the unexplained. It raises questions about the limits of medical knowledge during that era and our human tendency to weave tales that blur the line between reality and imagination.

## SUDOKU SEIZURES

Sudoku, the beloved number puzzle game, has been a source of leisure and mental exercise for millions. However, for a small group of people, playing Sudoku can trigger something bizarre and unexpected: seizures. Seizures are sudden, uncontrolled electrical disturbances in the brain that can lead to a variety of physical symptoms, including twitching, muscle spasms, and involuntary movements.

The phenomenon was first documented in 2008 when a 25-year-old man in Germany experienced a seizure while working on a Sudoku puzzle. The man had previously been buried by an avalanche while skiing and had spent fifteen minutes with an insufficient flow of oxygen in his body.

As a result, parts of his brain were damaged and he had to endure a long rehabilitation process, but eventually made a full recovery. However, something strange happened one day. While the man was working on solving a Sudoku puzzle, his left arm suddenly started seizing – the muscles contracting and shifting involuntarily. As soon as he stopped solving the puzzle, the seizures inexplicably stopped as well.

Researchers had never heard of sudoku-induced epilepsy before, and began to explore the condition. It soon became clear that it was a case of reflex epilepsy – a condition where seizures are triggered by specific things that happen outside the body, like puzzles, reading, calculations, and even touching certain things at specific temperatures. Interestingly, for this particular man, even similar things like reading, writing, or making math calculations did not lead to seizures. Only Sudoku.

Luckily, once he stopped solving Sudokus, the seizures stopped and never returned. Think about that the next time you see the daily puzzle in the newspaper!

## THE WILDEST WEST

In the early 20th century, the small town of Palisade, Nevada, faced a common challenge of many small towns—declining population and economic struggles. However, the resourceful residents of Palisade had a unique idea to breathe new life into their community. They decided to create their own version of the Wild West, a popular theme at the time, to attract visitors and capture the spirit of adventure.

The townspeople transformed Palisade into a living, breathing Wild West spectacle. They recreated scenes from the era, featuring cowboys, outlaws, and even Native American tribes. Buildings were restored to resemble the Old West, complete with saloons, jails, and shops. The town's residents dressed in period attire and staged mock shootouts and horseback chases for the entertainment of visitors.

Palisade's Wild West show was a hit, drawing tourists from near and far who were eager to experience the excitement of the frontier. The town's invention of the Wild West was a clever way to boost tourism and inject new energy into the local economy. It offered visitors a taste of the adventurous spirit that defined the American frontier.

Over time, however, the Wild West spectacle in Palisade faded away. As the years went by, interest waned, and the town's unique experiment gradually came to an end. Today, Palisade is a quiet and peaceful place, a reminder of its colorful past as a Wild West haven.

# FROM HOLLYWOOD TO WORLD WAR II

Hedy Lamarr, known for her roles in classic films, was not just a glamorous actress—she was also an inventor with a remarkable impact on the world and technology. During World War II, Lamarr and composer George Antheil teamed up to create a groundbreaking invention known as "frequency hopping spread spectrum technology".

This invention aimed to solve a critical problem faced by the Allies: the jamming of radio-controlled torpedoes by enemy forces. Lamarr and Antheil's solution involved using a system that rapidly changed radio frequencies, making it extremely difficult for enemies to interfere with communication between torpedoes and ships.

The duo's innovative idea combined Lamarr's knowledge of the entertainment industry (she had previously studied film and engineering) with Antheil's expertise in music. They developed a system that hopped between 88 different frequencies, inspired by the way Antheil's piano used synchronized paper rolls to create music.

Sadly, it wasn't until years later that their frequency-hopping invention gained recognition for its potential applications in military and civilian communications.

While Hedy Lamarr's wartime invention may not have been immediately embraced, her legacy as an inventor and innovator continues to inspire. The technology she helped develop laid the foundation for modern technologies like Wi-Fi, Bluetooth, and GPS.

Lamarr's story is a reminder that intelligence and creativity can thrive in unexpected places. Her contributions to science and technology go beyond the silver screen, showcasing the power of women in shaping history.

# THE REAL POCAHONTAS

You might have watched the animated movie "Pocahontas" and enjoyed its catchy songs and captivating storyline. But did you know it was based on a real story?

Pocahontas was a member of the Powhatan tribe, a Native American group living in what is now Virginia. She was born around 1596 and her given name was Matoaka. The events of her life were quite different from the animated Disney movie.

In reality, Pocahontas was a bridge between the Native American and English settlers. She is famously known for saving the life of Englishman John Smith. According to historical accounts, Pocahontas intervened when her father, Chief Powhatan, was about to execute Smith. Her actions established a temporary truce between the Powhatan tribe and the settlers.

Pocahontas later married Englishman John Rolfe, which helped establish a period of relative peace between the Powhatan tribe and the English colonists. The couple traveled to England, where Pocahontas was Baptized and became known as Rebecca Rolfe.

The Disney movie "Pocahontas," released in 1995, was inspired by the historical figure but took creative liberties to create an engaging story for audiences. In the movie, Pocahontas is portrayed as a free-spirited and adventurous young woman who befriends John Smith and fights for the harmony between her tribe and the settlers. While the movie captures some elements of Pocahontas' spirit, it doesn't fully depict the complexities of her life and the challenges faced by both Native Americans and settlers.

# NICARAGUAN SIGN LANGUAGE

In the 1980s, researchers noticed something remarkable and bizarre happening in Nicaragua. A community of deaf individuals, who had never been exposed to formal sign language, were creating their own unique system of communication. This phenomenon became known as Nicaraguan Sign Language (NSL).

NSL's emergence was a result of deaf children coming together in schools and forming a community. Initially, these children used simple gestures to communicate. However, as they interacted and shared experiences, they began to develop more complex and structured signs to express their thoughts and ideas, all without speaking a single word. A language was born from nothing, with thousands of people spanning generations adopting and learning a full vocabulary and set of grammatical rules.

What's truly remarkable about NSL is that it was created by its users, not imposed by any authority. As new generations of deaf children joined the community, they learned and contributed to this evolving language. The children adapted and expanded their vocabulary and grammar, making NSL more sophisticated over time.

The emergence of NSL provided researchers with a unique opportunity to study the birth and evolution of a language. It showcased the innate human capacity for communication and language development, even in the absence of a formal language model. As linguists studied NSL, they gained insights into how languages are structured, how they evolve, and how they are passed down through generations.

## THE FAKE PRINCE OF TAIWAN

Born sometime around 1679, George Psalmanazar's life story is a mixture of deception, creativity, and a thirst for adventure.

Psalmanazar began his life in France, but he would eventually become known for his elaborate masquerade as a native of Formosa (modern-day Taiwan). At a young age, he embarked on a journey of self-invention, crafting a persona that captured the curiosity of people across Europe.

In the early 18th century, Psalmanazar arrived in London, where he claimed to be a prince from the distant island of Formosa. He spun tales of a unique culture, customs, and language, captivating audiences with his descriptions of a faraway land. Psalmanazar's ruse even included a complete fictional alphabet and language.

His invented identity gained attention and even led to the publication of a book titled "An Historical and Geographical Description of Formosa," where he detailed the customs and way of life of his supposed homeland. People were captivated by his stories, and he became a sort of celebrity, holding lectures and demonstrations about Formosan culture.

However, as time went on, Psalmanazar's charade began to unravel. Scholars and experts began to question the authenticity of his claims, and eventually, he admitted that his tales of Formosa were a fabrication, revealing that he was actually a poor Frenchman named Esprit-Antoine de Flechier.

While Psalmanazar's deception may have left some disappointed, his story remains a testament to the power of imagination and the allure of the unknown. His ability to create an entire fictional identity, complete with language and culture, was a remarkable feat of creativity and storytelling.

## THE LOST COLONY OF ROANOKE

In the late 16th century, English explorers set their sights on establishing colonies in the New World. One such colony was established on Roanoke Island, off the coast of what is now North Carolina. Led by explorer John White, this group of settlers aimed to build a new life in the untamed wilderness.

However, the colony faced numerous challenges from the start. Supplies were scarce, and relations with local Native American tribes were often strained. In 1587, John White sailed back to England to secure additional resources for the struggling colony. But when he returned in 1590, a chilling discovery awaited him—the entire settlement had vanished without a trace.

The only clue left behind was the word "CROATOAN" carved into a post and "CRO" etched into a nearby tree. These cryptic messages hinted at the possibility that the settlers might have sought refuge with the local Croatoan tribe. However, despite efforts to locate the missing colonists, their fate remained shrouded in mystery.

The fate of the Lost Colony of Roanoke has given rise to countless theories and speculation. Some think that the settlers integrated with the Croatoan tribe, while others propose that they were attacked by hostile Native American groups. Some believe the colonists might even have attempted to sail back to England but were lost at sea.

The lack of concrete evidence has only fueled the allure of the story, leaving us to wonder about the fate of those early settlers and the challenges they faced in a new and unfamiliar land.

## THE MYSTERY OF THE TAOS HUM

In the town of Taos, New Mexico, a strange humming sound has been reported by a number of people for decades. This hum is so faint that it can't be heard by everyone—only a select few individuals seem to perceive it. Imagine hearing a distant, persistent drone that's not coming from any obvious source, like traffic or machinery.

The Taos Hum is a perplexing mystery because no one can pinpoint its exact origin. Some have speculated that it might be caused by industrial equipment, power lines, or even geological activity deep within the Earth. However, no conclusive evidence has been found to explain the strange phenomenon.

Those who claim to hear the Taos Hum describe it as a nuisance that can interfere with their daily lives. Some people have even reported experiencing physical discomfort or anxiety due to the unrelenting sound.

Scientists have attempted to study the Taos Hum, using specialized equipment to detect and measure the mysterious noise. However, these efforts have yielded mixed results, leaving the origin of the hum still shrouded in uncertainty. Some researchers suggest that the hum might be a form of tinnitus, a condition where individuals perceive sounds that aren't actually present.

## THE DISAPPEARANCE OF THE USS CYCLOPS

In March 1918, during World War I, the USS Cyclops, a massive ship, set out from Brazil towards Baltimore, Maryland. Laden with manganese ore and carrying over 300 crew members, the ship was an essential part of the war effort. However, it never reached its destination and vanished without a trace.

The disappearance of the USS Cyclops is particularly puzzling due to the circumstances surrounding its vanishing. There were no distress signals, no reports of bad weather, and no evidence of enemy action. One minute it was there, and then suddenly – it wasn't.

Over the years, numerous theories have been proposed to explain the ship's disappearance. Some suggest that it was the victim of a sudden storm or a rogue wave that caused it to capsize. Others speculate that a coal explosion might have occurred on board, leading to a catastrophic event that sunk the ship.

Another theory that gained traction is the connection to the Bermuda Triangle—a region infamous for mysterious disappearances of ships and aircraft. While the Bermuda Triangle theory adds an air of intrigue to the mystery, there is no concrete evidence to confirm this explanation.

Despite extensive searches and investigations, the fate of the USS Cyclops remains a mystery. The lack of wreckage, debris, or any indication of what happened to the ship has only deepened the enigma. The sudden and complete disappearance of such a large vessel continues to captivate the imagination and fuel speculation.

## THE WOW! SIGNAL

It's August 15, 1977, and astronomer Dr. Jerry R. Ehman is at Ohio State University's Big Ear radio telescope, routinely scanning the sky to detect radio signals from distant galaxies. For most of the night, all he notices is the usual static noise that's commonly picked up by radio telescopes. But then, something extraordinary happens. For just over one minute, 72 seconds to be exact, the telescope records an incredibly strong radio signal from the constellation Sagittarius. In his notes, Dr. Ehman circles the signal and writes "Wow!" in the margin. Little did he know that this would become one of the most famous mysteries in the history of space exploration—the Wow! signal.

Despite many attempts to detect it, the Wow! signal has never been observed again since that August night. Scientists believe it could have been a signal from an extraterrestrial civilization, a one-time burst of energy from a distant star, or maybe something as simple and underwhelming as interference from a passing satellite.

What made the Wow! signal intriguing was its incredible strength – 30 times louder than the regular background noise. This indicated that it came from a powerful source. The signal was also very narrow in frequency, kind of like a laser beam. This is part of the reason scientists think the signal might indicate communication from an extraterrestrial source – because narrow frequency is more common in artificial signals than natural cosmic noise.

The Wow! signal remains one of the greatest mysteries in the field of astronomy. Whether it was a message from an extraterrestrial civilization or just a natural cosmic phenomenon, the Wow! signal will continue to "wow" us until maybe, someday, it is once again detected.

## THE VANISHING VILLAGE OF ANGIKUNI

The Inuit village of Angikuni in Canada's Nunavut territory appeared to be a typical Arctic settlement. Nestled against the frozen landscape, it was a place where indigenous people lived off the land and relied on traditional ways of life.

However, in November 1930, a fur trapper named Joe Labelle arrived in Angikuni only to find it completely deserted. The village, which was home to around 2,000 people, showed no signs of life. The fires in the homes were still burning, food was left uneaten on the tables, and personal belongings remained behind.

The disappearance of an entire village raised alarm bells, and the search for answers began. Yet, no trace of the villagers was ever found. The Inuit had left behind their sled dogs, a crucial part of their way of life, which was highly unusual.

Speculation about what happened to the villagers of Angikuni has given rise to numerous theories. Disease or famine may have forced the Inuit to abandon their village in search of better conditions. Perhaps even supernatural forces or extraterrestrial beings may have played a role in their disappearance.

Despite extensive investigations, to this day no one knows what happened to the Angikuni villagers. The mystery is a haunting reminder of the many unknowns that exist in our world, especially in places as remote and secluded as the Arctic Circle.

## PERU'S NAZCA LINES

If you fly over the Nazca Desert in Peru, you might notice gigantic shapes coming into focus below you. In 1926, Peruvian archaeologist Toribio Mejia Xesspe began studying these gigantic, intricate, ancient drawings etched into the earth's surface across the Nazca Desert.

The Nazca Lines were created by the ancient Nazca people, who lived in the region from around 200 BCE to 600 CE. These massive drawings—ranging from simple lines to complex animals, plants, and geometric shapes—were carved into the desert floor by removing the reddish-brown iron oxide-coated pebbles to reveal the lighter-colored earth beneath.

What makes the Nazca Lines so fascinating is their colossal size and the precision with which they were crafted. Some of the "geoglyphs," as they are called, are over 1,000 feet long and can only be fully appreciated from the sky or nearby hilltops. How did the ancient Nazca people create these intricate designs with such accuracy, given the limited technology of their time?

The purpose behind the Nazca Lines remains shrouded in mystery. Some theories suggest that they were used for ceremonial or religious purposes, or served as a form of communication or navigation aids. Additionally, some researchers believe that the lines may have been part of astronomical rituals or water rituals tied to the region's limited water supply.

Regardless of their purpose, their stunning beauty and the enigmatic stories they tell of ancient cultures have turned the Nazca Desert into a living archaeological puzzle.

## THE BALLOON HOAX

Edgar Allen Poe is best known for his dark and mysterious works of literature. But perhaps one of his most shocking pieces of work was not literature at all – but a practical joke.

In 1844, the New York Sun newspaper published a shocking and sensational story that captivated readers far and wide. The headline read:

ASTOUNDING NEWS!

THE ATLANTIC CROSSED IN THREE DAYS!

SIGNAL TRIUMPH OF MR. MONCK MASON'S FLYING MACHINE!!!

Now, keep in mind that this was decades before the first airplane was built. The article claimed that European balloonist Monck Mason had crossed the Atlantic Ocean in only 75 hours in a flying gas balloon. The article featured diagrams and sketches of the aircraft.

The article was so convincing that readers far and wide were certain that a truly miraculous feat had been accomplished. However, it was soon revealed that the entire story was a fabrication—a hoax designed to capture the public's attention and boost newspaper sales. The author behind this imaginative tale was none other than Edgar Allan Poe, master of suspense and creativity.

Poe was supposedly inspired by a similar hoax printed in the same newspaper ten years earlier, claiming that life had been observed on the moon.

## LIGHTS OVER PHOENIX

On October 28, 2011, during a high school football game in Phoenix Arizona, hundreds of people observed a fascinating sight in the night sky – four bright lights, moving slowly through the sky above the stadium, blinking in and out again, and then disappearing completely after just a minute and a half.

Theories abounded about what had caused the lights to appear, with the most popular theory involving extraterrestrial spacecraft. Videos of the lights were uploaded to YouTube, the story hit the news outlets, and people everywhere were perplexed by the strange phenomenon.

However, in the end, the answer is probably far less exciting than alien UFOs. It turns out that on the same evening, an Arizona-based skydiving team was holding an annual Halloween event which included jumping out of an airplane holding bright flares, for a spectacularly spooky exhibition. The skydivers were actually quite far from the stadium, however due to a clear sky and optimal weather conditions, they could be seen as far away as from the school.

That was not the first time there had been suspected UFO activity in Phoenix's skies. In 1997 there had been a similar incident of bright lights appearing in the sky. This had later turned out to have been related to a military training exercise at a nearby air force base.

## MYSTERY OF THE MARY CELESTE

In December 1872, the Mary Celeste, an American merchant ship, set sail from New York to Genoa, Italy, carrying a cargo of alcohol. However, when another ship, the Dei Gratia, spotted the Mary Celeste floating adrift near the Azores islands, it became clear that something was amiss. The ship was in perfect condition, but the crew was nowhere to be found – it was empty.

The mystery of the Mary Celeste deepened as investigators boarded the ship. All signs pointed to a hasty departure—meals were strewn about half-eaten, personal belongings were left behind, and even the crew's personal papers remained on board. The ship's lifeboat was missing, making them think that some crew members may have abandoned ship.

Theories abound about what might have happened to the crew of the Mary Celeste. Some suggest that they may have encountered rough weather that forced them to abandon ship in a panic. Others speculate that the cargo of alcohol might have leaked fumes, leading to an explosion or fire that prompted the crew to evacuate.

Despite extensive investigations and theories, the true fate of the Mary Celeste's crew remains unknown. The ship's eerie abandonment has led to stories of ghostly encounters and supernatural occurrences, adding an air of mystery to an already enigmatic tale.

## REPORTER SPY

Otto von Bismarck, a masterful statesman from Germany, was known for his skillful political maneuvering and diplomacy. He was instrumental in the unification of Germany in the late 19th century and served as the first Chancellor of the German Empire.

Henri de Blowitz, on the other hand, was a prominent journalist hailing from France. Known for his role as a reporter for "The Times" in London, Blowitz had an uncanny ability to gather information and uncover secrets. He became famous for his accurate predictions and inside scoops on international affairs, earning him the nickname "The Prince of Reporters."

The intersection of their stories occurred during the Balkan Crisis of 1875-1878, a period of political tension and unrest in Europe. Bismarck, with his deep understanding of international politics, was trying to prevent a larger conflict from erupting. Meanwhile, Blowitz was stationed in Vienna, using his journalistic skills to gather information and provide insights into the diplomatic negotiations.

Blowitz's ability to out-scoop diplomats and intelligence agents and predict future political moves was well known. So Bismarck, concerned that Blowitz would predict his plans to redraw certain European borders and release them to the media, hired a spy to report on Blowitz's activities. But the spy had a problem – no matter how hard he tried, he could not find anything suspicious about what Blowitz was doing.

Yet, somehow, the information kept getting out and leaking to the press. It was later revealed that Blowitz had been working with a man on the inside, and the two had been using a hat to exchange messages between them. Essentially, Henri de Blowitz was the first reporter to out-spy an actual spy.

## PIGEONS AT WAR

When World War I raged across Europe, communications were carefully monitored by authorities to intercept any covert or espionage operations. So, a new method of getting important military messages through had to be developed.

Messenger pigeons, also known as homing pigeons, proved to be an ingenious solution. These intelligent birds possessed an innate ability to find their way back to their home from even hundreds of miles away, making them ideal messengers in treacherous conditions.

As the war raged on, messenger pigeons were used by various countries, including the United States, the United Kingdom, and Germany. Pigeons were often carried by aircraft or parachuted into enemy territory, where they would be released to return with crucial messages.

One famous story involves a pigeon named Cher Ami, who served with the U.S. Army Signal Corps. During the Battle of Verdun, Cher Ami delivered a message that saved nearly 200 soldiers by providing their coordinates and requesting artillery support. Despite being wounded in the process, Cher Ami completed the mission and became a celebrated hero.

Messenger pigeons faced extraordinary challenges during their missions. They had to navigate through gunfire, harsh weather, and even enemy attacks. Some pigeons were even equipped with small cameras to capture aerial photographs, further aiding military intelligence. These brave little messengers made a real difference, becoming true war heroes.

## THE GREAT EMU WAR

The year was 1932, and the stage was set in Western Australia. In the aftermath of World War I, many Australian veterans were given land to farm as part of a government initiative. These veterans had received land to grow wheat, but little did they know that they were about to face an unanticipated adversary – the emu.

Emus, large flightless birds native to Australia, had multiplied in significant numbers, becoming a menace to the wheat fields. As they descended upon the farmlands in search of food, they trampled crops and caused considerable damage. Frustrated farmers saw their efforts to cultivate wheat thwarted by the unrelenting emu hordes.

In a perplexing twist of events, the farmers called upon the Australian government for assistance. In an effort to protect their livelihoods, the government dispatched Major G.P.W. Meredith and a small group of soldiers armed with two Lewis machine guns. Their mission: to cull the emu population and put an end to the agricultural havoc.

The stage was now set for an unusual showdown between human technology and nature's feathered inhabitants. As the soldiers arrived, they faced the challenge of targeting fast-moving emus across vast, open terrain. The emus, however, proved to be agile and elusive opponents, often scattering in different directions when the soldiers attempted to fire.

The emus' survival instincts and swift movements made the operation more complex than anticipated. Despite their firepower, the soldiers struggled to effectively reduce the emu population. The media caught wind of the peculiar conflict, and headlines around the world began to share the unlikely tale of humans waging war against birds.

As days turned into weeks, it became apparent that the battle was not going as planned. The emus adapted to the soldiers' tactics, dodging bullets and evading capture. Public sentiment began to shift, and sympathy for the emus grew. The absurdity of the situation captured the imagination of many, and the government's efforts were met with ridicule.

Ultimately, after several weeks of struggle, the government decided to withdraw its troops, acknowledging that the emus had emerged victorious in the Great Emu War.

The Great Emu War has become a quirky piece of Australian history, a tale that showcases the sometimes unpredictable and humorous interactions between humans and the animal kingdom. Today, the story is remembered with a mix of amusement and bewilderment, and it serves as a reminder that even the most well-intentioned efforts can lead to unexpected outcomes.

## THE CHRISTMAS TRUCE

It was Christmas Eve in 1914 and World War I had been raging for several months. Soldiers from various different nations found themselves in brutal and grueling battles along the Western Front in Europe, many far from home and the festivities Christmas usually brought with it.

On that Christmas Eve, British and German soldiers were entrenched not far apart, when the British soldiers suddenly noticed something strange. There were candles burning outside the German trenches, flickering happily with holiday cheer. Then, carol singing began. The young men, separated by the trenches, were far from home and family, and something about the festive occasion made them put down their arms and choose to sing instead.

Bravely, the soldiers crossed the No Man's Land, the distance between the trenches, and exchanged Christmas greetings and even gifts. Tobacco, food, and alcohol were passed around and the battleground quieted as the men sat down and celebrated together.

Some accounts even tell of impromptu soccer matches breaking out, with soldiers using their helmets as goalposts.

However, the truce was short-lived. Commanding officers on both sides were not pleased with the fraternization and ordered their troops back to their trenches. The war resumed, and the Christmas Truce became no more than a fleeting moment of humanity in the midst of a brutal war.

# D-DAY GIRLS

When we think of heroes in World War II, we often picture soldiers on the front lines or pilots in the skies. However, the real heroes of war come in many forms, and during World War II, a group of remarkable women emerged as unsung heroes – the D-Day Girls.

In the early 1940s, as Europe faced the advance of German Nazi forces, the British Special Operations Executive (SOE) formed a secret army of courageous women to manage the fight behind enemy lines. These women would become spies, saboteurs, and radio operators, working undercover to aid the resistance movements in Nazi-occupied territories.

The SOE launched a covert recruitment campaign for women who possessed exceptional qualities, including courage, resourcefulness, and the ability to remain calm under pressure. They received training in sabotage, combat, and espionage techniques. These women became known as the D-Day Girls.

After completing their training, they were deployed to European countries, including France, where they played a vital role in preparing for the Allied invasion of Normandy, known as D-Day. They often disguised themselves as locals, blending into their surroundings.

One of the most critical roles these women undertook was that of radio operators. They transmitted vital information about enemy movements and other intelligence back to Allied forces in England. Operating behind enemy lines, their work was extremely dangerous; they were at constant risk of being captured.

Despite the incredible bravery and contribution of the D-Day Girls, their stories remained largely untold for decades. It was only in recent years that their heroic deeds received the recognition they deserved. These women truly are unsung heroes of World War II, and their legacy will continue to inspire generations to come.

## HITLER'S FROZEN NAZI BASE

Amid the tumultuous years of World War II, rumors emerged of a secret Nazi base nestled within the frozen landscapes of Antarctica. The story suggests that high-ranking Nazi officials, including Adolf Hitler himself, had constructed a hidden fortress known as "Base 211" or the "Nazi Base in Antarctica." This remote location was believed to house advanced technology, research facilities, and perhaps even an escape route for Nazi leaders.

However, as captivating as this narrative may be, historians and researchers have found little concrete evidence to support the existence of such a base. While some conspiracy theories speculate about hidden tunnels and advanced weaponry beneath the ice, the truth is more elusive.

One significant challenge to the existence of the secret Nazi base is the harsh environment of Antarctica. The extreme cold, treacherous terrain, and logistical difficulties of maintaining such a base in secrecy make the story seem implausible. Moreover, most historical records indicate that Hitler's focus was primarily on European conquest and not on establishing a remote base on a distant continent.

So where did the story come from? The origins of the Nazi Antarctic base myth can be traced back to post-World War II years when various speculations arose about the Nazis' mysterious activities. While some theories were based on genuine research expeditions, others were fueled by sensationalism and conspiracy.

Modern expeditions to Antarctica have uncovered no concrete evidence of hidden structures or technological installations. Satellite imagery and archaeological investigations have failed to support the claims of a substantial Nazi presence.

# CORRIE TEN BOOM

Growing up in a loving and devoutly Christian family in Haarlem, Netherlands, Corrie ten Boom was taught the values of kindness and empathy from a young age. Her family ran a watchmaker's shop in Haarlem, and they were deeply committed to helping those in need.

As the clouds of World War II gathered over Europe, the ten Boom family made a courageous decision. They turned their home into a hiding place for Jewish people fleeing the horrors of the Holocaust. Their secret room, concealed behind a false wall, became a sanctuary for those seeking refuge from the Nazis.

Corrie and her family risked their lives to save nearly 800 Jewish individuals from persecution and almost certain death. Their heroic efforts came with constant danger, as the Nazis intensified their search for Jews and those who aided them. Corrie learned to trust her instincts and rely on her faith during these perilous times.

In 1944, the ten Boom family's secret was discovered, and they were arrested by the Gestapo. Corrie was sent to the notorious Ravensbrück concentration camp in Germany. Life in the camp was unimaginably harsh, yet even in this bleak place, her faith and compassion continued to shine.

In December 1944, miraculously, due to a clerical error, Corrie was released from the camp. After her release, Corrie dedicated her life to sharing her story and spreading the message of forgiveness and reconciliation. She wrote a book, "The Hiding Place," which detailed her family's brave actions and her experiences during the war. Corrie traveled the world, speaking about the power of forgiveness and the importance of faith in the face of adversity.

# THE GHOST ARMY

Like the D-Day Girls, the Ghost Army was another secret unit that had a huge impact on the outcome of World War II, whose members used deception and illusion to outwit the enemy.

The Ghost Army was officially known as the 23rd Headquarters Special Troops, and it was composed of a diverse group of artists, actors, and sound engineers. Their mission was to mislead and confuse the enemy by creating the illusion of a much larger Allied force than actually existed.

The Ghost Army did not have real tanks, but they had inflatable ones. These were made to look so convincing that even experienced enemy spies were fooled. They would inflate faux tanks, trucks, and artillery pieces behind the front lines, creating the illusion of a massive army ready to attack. The Ghost Army employed audio deception as well. They used powerful speakers to broadcast the sounds of a large and active military unit, including tanks rumbling, soldiers talking, and artillery firing.

They would even leave behind cigarette butts and other items to make it appear as though a large number of soldiers had recently passed through.

In the Battle of the Bulge in 1944, the Ghost Army created the illusion of an entire army group with just a few hundred men. They set up phony headquarters, complete with radio traffic and even sent fake coded messages. This successfully diverted German forces away from the actual Allied offensive.

The Ghost Army's work was incredibly dangerous. They often operated close to the front lines, and if the enemy had discovered their true nature, the consequences could have been dire. Yet, their clever deceptions saved countless lives by diverting enemy attention and preventing them from reinforcing their positions.

## THE NIGHT WITCHES

During World War II, a group of fearless women earned a nickname that struck fear into the hearts of their enemies: the Night Witches. These women were part of an all-female Soviet bomber regiment that flew daring nighttime missions.

The Night Witches got their eerie nickname from the German soldiers they fought against, who believed that the sound of the Soviet planes resembled the swooshing of a witch's broomstick.

What made the Night Witches unique was not just their spooky nickname, but also their remarkable bravery and determination. These women flew slow and outdated Polikarpov Po-2 biplanes, which were little more than canvas and wood. They were not equipped with the powerful weapons or heavy armor of other military aircraft.

The Night Witches' missions were perilous. They had to contend with anti-aircraft fire, difficult weather conditions, and the constant threat of enemy fighter planes. They would often cut their engines to glide in silence, making it difficult for the enemy to detect their approach until it was too late.

Along with defying gender roles far before their time, the Night Witches' contribution to the war was significant. They flew more than 30,000 missions and dropped over 23,000 tons of bombs on the enemy. Their relentless night raids disrupted the Axis forces, making them a formidable and feared adversary.

## TOOTSIE ROLLS IN KOREA

During the Korean War, the American First Marine Division was stationed out in the freezing cold among the North Korean mountains. Communicating via radio, they would use unique call signs to prevent their enemies from interpreting and understanding their strategies and tactics, so all sorts of tactical words were assigned code names.

One particularly freezing night, the Marines called over the radio asking for ammunition and used the code name – tootsie rolls. But the radio operator on the other side must have missed a lesson because it turned out he had no idea that "tootsie rolls" actually meant ammunition! So what did he do? He sent planes loaded with actual tootsie rolls to fly over the Marines and parachute the treats from the sky.

The hilarious mistake actually worked out fine, as the tootsie rolls provided much-needed nourishment for the hungry troops. Although they were out of ammunition, they discovered that the tootsie rolls were a great resource in battle – in addition to being eaten, they could be warmed and softened and then used as makeshift bandages to stop bleeding until wounded soldiers could be evacuated, or used to repair damaged equipment.

With their equipment fixed and their wounds under control, the troops managed to collect their injured and frostbitten comrades, fought through the enemy lines, and finally retreated to safety.

## THE WELBIKE

During World War II, military ingenuity produced a wide array of innovative solutions to the challenges of warfare. One such marvel was the Welbike, a compact and foldable motorcycle that played a significant role in the war effort.

In the early 1940s, as World War II raged on, the need for portable and easily deployable transportation for paratroopers and other special forces increased. Traditional motorcycles were too heavy to be a practical solution for airborne troops, who needed something lightweight and compact.

The British military, always quick to adapt to new challenges, initiated a project to create a small, collapsible motorcycle. The result was the Welbike a marvel of engineering, designed to be a one-person, one-speed, collapsible motorcycle that could be packed into a parachute and then dropped alongside paratroopers for quick and easy access on the ground.

The Welbike weighed only 71 pounds and could be folded down to fit into a small container for airdrop. It could reach speeds of up to 30 miles per hour. While its speed was limited, it was invaluable for moving quickly behind enemy lines or navigating through rough terrain. Once production was completed, Welbikes were used in missions like the D-Day landings in Normandy and Operation Market Garden in the Netherlands.

Today, while no longer in production or use, the Welbike is considered a rare collector's item.

## DOLLY THE CLONE SHEEP

The concept of "cloning" belongs deep in the world of science fiction and futuristic technology. But, in fact, it is not so far-fetched as we might imagine. In 1996, a Scottish sheep named Dolly made headlines around the globe as the first successfully cloned mammal.

Dolly was no ordinary sheep. She was created through a process known as *somatic cell nuclear transfer*, which involved taking a cell from an adult sheep and using it to create an identical genetic copy. This groundbreaking experiment was conducted by scientists at the Roslin Institute in Scotland.

What made Dolly's birth even more extraordinary was that she was the first mammal to be cloned from an adult somatic cell. Prior to Dolly, scientists believed that cloning could only be accomplished using embryonic cells — cells that are found in a fetus before it is born. But Dolly's arrival changed everything.

First, scientists collected a somatic cell from a six-year-old sheep. This cell provided the genetic material necessary to create a new sheep. They then took an unfertilized egg cell from another sheep and removed its nucleus, which contains genetic information. The nucleus from the somatic cell was placed into the empty egg cell, creating a new, combined cell with the same genetic material as the adult sheep.

This newly formed cell was then developed into an embryo and implanted into a mother sheep, and after a normal pregnancy, Dolly was born. Dolly was an exact genetic copy of the sheep that was cloned.

Dolly's birth opened up exciting possibilities in the world of science and genetics. Scientists realized that cloning could be used not only in animals but potentially in humans as well. It also offered hope for preserving endangered species and even resurrecting extinct ones.

Dolly passed away in 2003, but her legacy lives on in the ongoing exploration of cloning and its applications in medicine, agriculture, and conservation.

## KOKO THE TALKING GORILLA

Language is something that we associate exclusively with humans. Sure, parrots can mimic people, but they don't really understand what they are saying, nor can they hold a conversation. But Koko the Gorilla is known as the first ever actual communicating animal.

Early in her life, Koko, who was born and lived at the San Francisco Zoo, was chosen to participate in an experiment by Dr. Francine Patterson, a psychologist with a passion for studying gorillas. Dr. Patterson began trying to teach Koko American Sign Language (ASL) as a way to bridge the gap between humans and gorillas and to explore their cognitive abilities.

As Koko grew, so did her signing skills. She managed to learn hundreds of signs and even created some of her own by combining existing signs in new ways. This demonstrated not only her capacity for learning but also her ability to think creatively.

Koko's linguistic achievements were impressive, but what truly set her apart was her emotional intelligence. She formed deep connections with both humans and other animals. One of her most famous friendships was with a kitten named All Ball, whom she cared for and loved. This touching relationship showed the world that animals, like humans, can be capable of empathy and compassion.

She could not only communicate about her immediate needs but also express abstract thoughts and emotions. For example, when her beloved pet kitten, All Ball, tragically died, Koko used sign language to convey her feelings of sadness and loss.

Koko became an icon, appearing on the cover of National Geographic and in numerous documentaries. People around the world admired her for her ability to express complex emotions through sign language. She was a symbol of hope for the conservation of gorillas, whose populations were dwindling due to habitat loss and poaching.

## UNSINKABLE SAM THE CAT

Cats are believed to have nine lives, but how many cats do you know who survived death twice?

Unsinkable Sam's remarkable tale begins during World War II. He was not an ordinary cat but a seafaring kitten aboard the German battleship Bismarck. Cats were a common presence on ships in those days, valued for their ability to deal with the ship's rat problem.

In May 1941, the Bismarck set sail on a mission in the Atlantic Ocean. However, unfortunately for them, the British Royal Navy located and engaged them in a fierce battle. During the intense fight, the ship was hit by British torpedoes and eventually sank. It seemed like Unsinkable Sam's first life had come to an end.

But Sam's incredible story didn't end there. He was found floating on a wooden plank amid the wreckage by the crew of the British destroyer HMS Cossack. Sam was adopted by the crew of the HMS Cossack, who affectionately named him "Oscar." He quickly became a beloved mascot and good luck charm for the ship. Sam sailed with the crew on various missions throughout the war. Then, in October 1941, tragedy struck once again. The

HMS Cossack was torpedoed by a German submarine and sank. This time, Sam was the only survivor among the crew, earning him the nickname "Unsinkable Sam."

After the war, Sam retired from his adventurous life at sea and lived out his remaining years in peace. Unsinkable Sam, the cat with three lives, will always be remembered as the incredible cat who survived against the odds.

## THE SEA LION GOLDEN GATE RESCUE

In the vast waters of San Francisco Bay, an extraordinary rescue unfolded that would forever change the life of a young man named Kevin Hines, and a sea lion who saved his life.

Kevin Hines was just 19 years old when he found himself standing on the edge of the Golden Gate Bridge. He made the fateful decision to jump, believing there was no hope left in the world. But fate had something unexpected in store for him.

As Kevin plummeted into the frigid waters of the bay, he felt an incredible force pulling at him. To his astonishment, a sea lion had come to his rescue. The sea lion swam beneath him, pushing him toward the surface.

Sea lions are known for their strong sense of curiosity and playfulness, but what happened next was nothing short of heroic. The sea lion kept Kevin until the Coast Guard arrived to rescue him.

Kevin was hurt from the fall, but he had been given a second chance at life. He went on to become an advocate for mental health awareness, sharing his own struggles with bipolar disorder and using his experience to inspire others to seek help when they're in crisis.

The heroic sea lion swam back off into the bay, but will always be remembered as a good friend to humans.

# ROSELLE THE 9/11 GUIDE DOG

On the fateful morning of September 11, 2001, amidst the chaos and terror that unfolded when the World Trade Center towers were attacked in New York City, a guide dog named Roselle became an unlikely hero.

Roselle had been trained by the Guide Dog Foundation for the Blind and was matched with Michael Hingson, a blind man, who worked on the 78th floor of the North Tower.

As the horrifying events of 9/11 unfolded, Michael and Roselle found themselves trapped in a smoke-filled stairwell, far above the ground. Despite the panic and confusion around them, Roselle knew her duty was to guide her owner to safety. She led Michael down 1,463 steps, all the way to the lobby of the North Tower.

Not only did Roselle know exactly what to do, but she helped Michael stay calm amid the uncertainty and chaos, and her sharp instincts guided them through the treacherous conditions of the burning building. Along the way, they encountered firefighters and first responders who were ascending the stairs to rescue those in need. They made a narrow escape, but both survived nonetheless.

In 2002, Roselle received the Dickin Medal, an award often referred to as the "Animal Victoria Cross," for her outstanding bravery and service on that fateful day.

# BALTO THE ALASKAN DOG

In January 1925, the town of Nome, Alaska, faced a grave health crisis. An outbreak of diphtheria, a highly contagious and potentially deadly disease, threatened the lives of many residents, especially children. The only hope for saving the town was to transport an antidote from the city of Anchorage, miles away, to Nome as quickly as possible.

The challenge was daunting. Temperatures were below freezing and blizzards had blocked off the roads or railways out of Nome.

A relay of dog sled teams was organized to carry the serum, with each team covering a portion of the treacherous journey. Balto, an Alaskan husky, was tasked with the leg before last, delivering the serum to the final point before Nome. However, when he and his "musher" (the dogsled driver) arrived at the meeting point, they discovered that the next team was nowhere to be found – so they decided to continue on, crossing the final leg of the distance, another 25 miles, through the winds and ice.

On February 2, 1925, Balto and his team finally arrived in Nome, carrying the precious serum that would save countless lives.

Balto's heroic journey made headlines across the country, and he became an instant hero. A statue was erected in his honor in New York City's Central Park, celebrating his bravery and the spirit of all the sled dogs who had participated in the Serum Run.

## THE PEABODY DUCKS

In the heart of downtown Memphis, Tennessee, a historic hotel is home to an unusual and charming tradition—the Peabody Ducks. These feathered friends have been waddling their way into the hearts of visitors for generations.

The story begins in the 1930s when the Peabody Hotel, a luxurious and elegant establishment, decided to add a touch of whimsy to its already opulent atmosphere. Legend has it that the general manager of the hotel, Frank Schutt, and a few of his friends had returned from a hunting trip and thought it would be amusing to place three of their live decoy ducks in the hotel's lobby fountain. It started as a joke – but the guests loved it!

Now, every day at 11 a.m., the Peabody Ducks make their grand entrance from their rooftop palace, a penthouse specially designed for their comfort. The "Duckmaster," a hotel employee who is in charge of the ducks, leads the procession. The red carpet is rolled out, and the ducks march down to the fountain, delighting visitors who gather to witness this unique spectacle.

The Peabody Ducks have become famous worldwide, attracting visitors from all corners of the globe. They have appeared on television shows, in books, and even in a movie. Their presence has added a touch of whimsy and warmth to the Peabody Hotel, making it a beloved landmark in Memphis.

## CHILLING CRIMES

## THE VANISHING OF D. B. COOPER

The Legend of D.B. Cooper is a real-life mystery that has puzzled experts and captured the imagination of people around the world.

In 1971, a man using the alias "Dan Cooper" (later mistakenly referred to as "D.B. Cooper") boarded a commercial airplane in Portland, Oregon. He calmly handed a note to a flight attendant, claiming he had a bomb and demanding $200,000 and parachutes. Once the demands were met, Cooper released the passengers at a remote location and instructed the crew to fly him to Mexico.

During the flight, Cooper donned a parachute and, with the money in hand, parachuted out of the rear stairway of the airplane over a wooded area near Washington's Cascade Mountains. He vanished into thin air, leaving behind a mystery that has never been fully solved.

Despite extensive investigations, the man's true identity and fate remain unknown. The story has sparked numerous theories, ranging from Cooper's survival and escape to his death in the harsh wilderness.

While some believe that Cooper could have successfully disappeared and lived under a new identity, others think that the elements and terrain would have made survival highly unlikely. The case has seen its fair share of hoaxes, copycat claims, and even amateur treasure hunters searching for clues.

Following three similar hijackings, the Federal Aviation Administration implemented a requirement that all Boeing 727 aircraft be fitted with a device known as the "Cooper Vane," a mechanical aerodynamic wedge, which prevents the rear stairway from being lowered in flight.

## FRIENDS WITH TED BUNDY

Ann Rule, a former Seattle police officer turned crime writer, had no idea that her path would cross with one of the most infamous criminals in history. She met Ted Bundy at a suicide hotline center where they both volunteered. Little did she know, Bundy would later become the subject of her book "The Stranger Beside Me."

As Ann Rule got to know Ted Bundy, she saw a charming and charismatic man who seemed to be the least likely candidate for a serial killer. However, as time went on, she couldn't ignore the growling suspicions and evidence that pointed to Bundy's involvement in a string of gruesome murders.

Ted Bundy would later go on to be accused of dozens of crimes, becoming notorious as one of the most prolific killers in America, and even in the world.

Rule's connection to Bundy became a chilling example of how even those closest to us can harbor dark secrets. Her struggle to reconcile the charming man she knew with the horrifying crimes he committed is a central theme in her book. Rule's unique perspective as both a friend and a crime writer added depth and insight to her narrative.

"The Stranger Beside Me" not only shed light on Bundy's crimes but also marked the beginning of Ann Rule's successful career as a true crime author. Her dedication to uncovering the truth behind the crimes, even when it meant confronting her own disbelief, made her work essential in the investigation and understanding of Bundy's atrocities.

# CATCH ME IF YOU CAN

You may have seen or heard of the movie, "Catch Me If You Can," starring Leonardo DiCaprio and Tom Hanks, about a young fraudster who conned and scammed his way through many years of his life. But did you know that the movie was based on a true story?

The real Frank Abagnale Jr. was born in 1948 and became one of the most famous con artists in history, known for his extraordinary ability to impersonate various professions and commit a series of ingenious frauds.

Frank was born in Bronxville, New York. At the age of 16, he ran away from home and embarked on a journey that would make him a legendary figure in the world of forgery and fraud.

Over several years, he posed as a Pan American World Airways pilot, a doctor, and a lawyer, among other professions. He used his fake identities to forge checks worth millions of dollars and travel the world without suspicion.

Abagnale's forgeries were so convincing that banks and businesses rarely questioned the authenticity of his checks. He used a combination of charm, confidence, and clever techniques to outsmart law enforcement at every turn.

Frank Abagnale's crimes eventually caught the attention of the FBI, and he found himself on the agency's most-wanted list. After several years of evading capture, Frank Abagnale was finally arrested in 1969 in France. He was extradited to the United States, where he faced a lengthy prison sentence. However, his remarkable skills caught the attention of the FBI, who offered him a deal: help them catch other forgers, and he would receive a reduced sentence.

Frank Abagnale accepted the FBI's offer and embarked on a new path as a consultant and lecturer. He used his insider knowledge to assist law enforcement agencies in combating fraud and forgery. Today, he is a respected authority on fraud prevention and has dedicated his life to helping others avoid the mistakes he made in his youth.

# A DARING ESCAPE FROM ALCATRAZ

Alcatraz was a formidable prison located on an island in San Francisco Bay, surrounded by chilly, treacherous waters. Considered inescapable, it was nicknamed "The Rock." From 1934 to 1963, only fourteen escape attempts were made, and most ended in failure. But one attempt, in 1962, remains a mystery to this day.

Three prisoners, Frank Lee Morris, Clarence Anglin, and John Anglin, concocted a brilliant plan to break free. Frank Morris already had a history of escaping from prison. He ended up at Alcatraz because of his numerous breakouts from other facilities.

Morris teamed up with brothers Clarence and John Anglin, who were also known for their escape skills. They had been sent to Alcatraz for crimes like bank robbery. Together with another inmate named Allen West, they devised an audacious escape plan.

First, they created fake heads out of papier-mâché, real hair clippings, and other materials. These heads were placed in their beds to trick the guards during nightly headcounts. Then, using makeshift tools, they chipped away slowly at the walls until they had made a hole large enough to exit through.

Once out of their cells, they crawled through a utility corridor with a raft they had secretly built from raincoats.

On the night of June 11, 1962, the three inflated their raft and paddled away into the dark waters of the bay. The escapees were never captured, nor were they seen alive again. Officially, they are listed as missing, presumed dead. Yet, some believe they might have survived. Although it's likely they didn't make it, the mystery lives on, making the Alcatraz escape one of history's most intriguing unsolved cases.

# THE SMILEY FACE KILLER

The "Smiley Face Killer" is a mysterious urban legend that has intrigued people for years.

In the late 1990s, authorities noticed a disturbing pattern: young college-aged men were disappearing and later found dead in bodies of water. The cases seemed to be completely unrelated, until someone noticed a creepy similarity: Painted or graffitied smiley face symbols near the locations where several of the bodies were found.

The smiley face graffiti, it was believed, was the killer's sinister signature. This theory quickly spread across the internet and in true crime circles, captivating the imaginations of many.

However, law enforcement officials have largely dismissed the Smiley Face Killer theory. They argue that the smiley face graffiti is likely coincidental, as smiley face symbols are common and found in many places. They insist that the deaths are tragic, unrelated accidents.

Still, the legend of the Smiley Face Killer endures. It has inspired books, documentaries, and even a few TV shows. Some amateur detectives continue to investigate the cases independently, convinced that there's more to the story than meets the eye.

## THE PIZZA KILLERS

In a quiet town in New Jersey, two teenagers, Jayson Vreeland and Thomas Koskovich, became the infamous "Pizza Killers." Their shocking crime left the community in disbelief and even today, no one really understands why they did what they did.

On April 19, 1995, Vreeland and Koskovich, just 17 and 18 years old at the time, called "Tony's Pizza and Pasta" and ordered two pizzas to be delivered to their home address. The pizzeria accepted their order and two pizza deliverymen, Jeremy Giordano and Giorgio Gallara, set out to deliver their pizzas.

Although the two teenagers did not know the men, for some strange reason, as soon as they pulled up at the house, Vreeland and Koskovitch attacked them in their car, shooting and killing them both.

The teens were arrested just two days after the murders and during their trial, revealed that "they had just always wanted to know what it was like to kill someone."

After both boys were found guilty, Vreeland was sent to a juvenile detention center and Koskovich was sentenced to death. To this day, there has been no real reason stated for why the pair carried out this horrific crime.

## THE MAN WHO SOLD THE EIFFEL TOWER

Victor Lustig was born in 1890 in Austria-Hungary. From a young age, he displayed a talent for manipulation and deceit. His life of crime began with small-time scams and forgeries, but he soon graduated to bigger and bolder cons.

One of Lustig's most infamous cons involved the iconic Eiffel Tower in Paris. In 1925, he read a newspaper article about the costly maintenance of the tower. Lustig saw an opportunity and decided to pose as a government official. He called together a group of scrap metal dealers and convinced them that the French government had decided to sell the Eiffel Tower for scrap metal due to financial difficulties.

One of the dealers was so convinced by Lustig's act that he paid him a large bribe to secure the deal. But once he had the money in hand, Lustig vanished, leaving his victim to realize that the whole scheme had been a lie. The dealer was so embarrassed that he did not report Lustig to the authorities, so Lustig returned to Paris – and carried out the entire scheme again. This audacious scheme earned Lustig the title of "The Man Who Sold the Eiffel Tower Twice."

Victor Lustig's criminal career came to an end when he made the mistake of conning an FBI agent in 1935. The agent, not fooled by Lustig's charm, arrested him. Lustig was eventually tried and sentenced to 20 years in prison for his various scams.

Thank you so much for reading
101 Interesting Stories About Everything!

I hope you learned a lot and enjoyed
the stories in this book.

We'd appreciate it so much if you would consider
going to Amazon and leaving a review.

Your reviews help us bring you more fun,
family-friendly content like this book.

# ABOUT MADE EASY PRESS

At Made Easy Press, our goal is to bring you beautifully designed, thoughtful gifts and products.

We strive to make complicated things – easy. Whether it's learning new skills or putting memories into words, our books are led by values of family, creativity, and self-care and we take joy in creating authentic experiences that make people truly happy.

Look out for other books
by Made Easy Press here!